G. CAMPBELL MORGAN
~ *Bible Teacher* ~

G. Campbell Morgan - Bible Teacher
This edition 1999

ISBN 1 84030 046 9

Ambassador Publications
a division of
Ambassador Productions Ltd.
Providence House
16 Hillview Avenue,
Belfast, BT5 6JR
Northern Ireland

Emerald House
1 Chick Springs Road, Suite 203
Greenville,
South Carolina 29609, USA
www.emeraldhouse.com

G. CAMPBELL MORGAN
~ *Bible Teacher* ~

HAROLD MURRAY

AMBASSADOR

BELFAST ◆ **GREENVILLE**
NORTHERN IRELAND   SOUTH CAROLINA

CONTENTS

CHAPTER I

Introductory—One Book—and many—Expositor and Evangelist—Dr. Morgan and Methodism—How he became a lay preacher—some milestones.

CHAPTER I

THERE must be no pretence about this little book.

It is not a biography of Dr. Campbell Morgan. That was done some years ago, and done well. It is not a collection of stories about a great preacher by a gossiping friend. It is merely a little tribute which he, who cares so little for the praise of men, will suffer for the sake, not only of those who know and love him, but for the sake of those, all over the world, who are interested in his life work.

I do not claim that there have been any special sittings for this rather hasty sketch, for there have not. All one hopes is that it may not be a caricature.

Now, men may be called to be preachers, prophets, or evangelists. Some of us have been called—and I use the word deliberately—to write about all three. After being in the calling for forty-five years, with hardly any other occupation, one can at least say it is one that has immense compensations. Some of my good friends who write constantly for what we call the religious press will know exactly what I mean when I say that while writing about beautiful pictures, or good books, or great sermons, is not to be compared for a moment with the supreme satisfaction of having tried to paint, write or preach them, it is a task which may be looked back upon with a certain satisfaction.

You see, you write a play; how soon it may be forgotten. You write of the lives say of film stars, or of great sportsmen, or of distinguished politicians; though interest may be aroused, nobody may be very much the better for it. You write about a preacher of the gospel, and you pass on to a wider congregation, words of his that may, perchance, echo in some hearts many a year afterwards, or may even immediately help and inspire some hungry soul.

I say it is a mightily agreeable task. Cheap publicity is hateful, especially where an ambassador of Christ gets it through anything but sound *preaching*. A publicity that will help to bring people to the Saviour he proclaims is never to be despised. Think of that, young and unassuming junior reporter, when you see your humble account of the Chapel meeting in the local paper.

Some odd word that you quote may save some-body, body and soul—if it were necessary I think I could argue that, with illustrations, for the rest of this book!

Well, in the course of the years I have written a good deal about Dr. Morgan. Not that he was a man whose reputation ever had anything at all to do with any sort of " boosting " ; people just wanted to read about him—as I know they still do.

And they never read much about such a man without getting some useful word from him. I expect I shall have to say something in this sketch of his appearance, and his style, but those things do not matter. It is what he has preached, his faithful, unchanging message, that counts.

Once more, with that touch of melancholy almost inevitable with advancing years, one reflects that the ranks grow fewer and fewer of those who can say they heard Moody, Spurgeon, Parker and other great preachers of their day. One cannot help wondering what names the young people of to-day will mention when they look back upon their early Church associations. There are so many able men known for all kinds of gifts. Sometimes their versatility is astonishing.

Not many stand out as Dr. Morgan does, as an *expository preacher*. Probably in fifty years to come the young folks of to-day will be talking mostly of men who first became popular through the radio which, with all its amazing influence can hardly be said to give Bible *teaching ;* many will be heard declaring : " I remember Campbell Morgan." In America, as in this country, they will be heard saying : " At Northfield, at Westminster, I sat at his feet, and he made the Bible a new book to me."

At the present time the stress is rightly being laid everywhere upon the need of evangelistic preaching. Most surely—and none would agree more heartily than Dr. Morgan—the evangelistic note must be sounded, not only wherever masses of men can be gathered in united gatherings, in churches and halls, but in the open air. Yet there is another side which is not, perhaps, emphasised as it should be. Anyone who has moved among the crowds in places like Hyde Park, as the writer has done for forty years, knows that thousands of men are prepared to believe in the existence of God, to reverence the name of Christ, but are hopelessly muddled regarding the Scriptures.

What many need is not so much an evangelistic appeal based on passages of Scripture but a clear, interesting, illuminating, convincing exposition of the Word that has been familiar to them from Sunday School days. They are confused by arguments in which partisans seek to dresent the view of a faction—" Our Church says so and so." Too rarely do they hear a man expounding God's Word. That is why one has pleaded in vain for a better representation of the Christian pulpit at such a forum as the Marble Arch, where there is so much wild, vehement shouting and so little sound teaching.

There never was a time when so many people, whether calling themselves disciples or not, were discussing the Bible, quoting the Bible, misquoting it, mutilating it, misconstruing it. In this critical age we need, above all, men who will stand up and say, " *Thus saith the Lord* ", men who have been given time for study of the Word, and are fitted to teach. Evangelist-Expositor—what a grand combination !

It is of such a man that I write.

In the British Museum Library you will find more than seventy books by Dr. Morgan. Some of them deal with everyday problems, but they are mostly for students. I am not dealing with a man who fritters away precious time in writing for sensational newspapers on topics of the town, pouring out cheap comment which is valued just to the extent to which it provides good headlines or a startling Sunday poster. Indeed, I do not know that Dr. Morgan has ever written for the Press. A great many of his sermons have been published. I fancy in practically every case they have been stenographically reported. I do not say " sermons and lectures " because really there is no difference between the two. A man may " lecture " on " My Cruise to Timbucktoo " or " Faces and Places " or something of that kind, but every Bible talk is a sermon.

You have only to look at the titles of some of the seventy or eighty books to gather the nature of the whole. I will not catalogue them, but here are one or two which have been in demand lately : " Great Chapters of the Bible ", " The Gospel According to John ", " Hosea, the Heart and Holiness of God ", " The Answers of

Jesus to Job ", " The Great Physician " (Fifty
studies which show Jesus at work, dealing with
individuals). The list includes " The Analysed
Bible ", in ten volumes, " The Study and
Teaching of The English Bible ", " Messages
of the Books of the Bible ", " The Bible and
the Child ", and others of the same kind.

I have been looking at one book, " Search-
lights from the Word ", published in America,
which contains no fewer than 1,188 sermon
suggestions, one from every chapter in the Bible.
These notes were written over a period of three
and a half years, and were published in a weekly
religious journal.

In an illuminating book recently published
the doctor has dealt with the whole subject of
preaching. It has never been his habit to preach
on current events. There are, of course, times
when from the pulpit the prophetic voice must
sound in some national or international situation.
At such a time, as he says, he has never had
to go anywhere but to the Bible for his
message.

Although he is never happier than when he
is expounding the Scriptures to a company of
Christian people, who sit before him with Bible

and notebook, and while most certainly he would not choose what may be described as special occasions for the particular exercise of his ministry, yet when such occasions demand his attention he rises to a great height of spiritual power and influence.

This was notably the case on the Sunday following the death of King George V. Dr. Morgan never forgets that Buckingham Palace, as he smilingly remarks, "is in his parish", and on this particular Sunday he thought of the sorrowing Queen and her family as though they were members of his own congregation. With deep feeling and rare insight, he referred to the King's life and work, drawing attention especially to His Majesty's love for and commendation of the Bible, and enforcing many lessons from a long and successful reign, for the benefit of those in the congregation. It is interesting to note that a copy of this sermon, suitably printed and bound, was accepted by Queen Mary, who caused a gracious message of appreciation to be sent to Dr. Morgan, a message which he highly prizes.

Something similar took place on the Coronation of King George VI when very large congregations assembled at Westminster on Coronation Sunday. With Biblical history as a background for his theory of kingship, Dr. Morgan emphasised the place that a modern sovereign could have in the life of his people. Those who listened to both these sermons came to the conclusion that although the famous preacher at Westminster would not choose special occasions, yet when these demands were made upon him, he was enabled to discharge such responsibilities with great spiritual power.

From 1886 onwards Dr. Morgan kept a record from which at his recent Diamond Jubilee he found he had preached 23,390 times. (You may now add more than a hundred to that.) In his sermons and lectures he has dealt with every Book in the Bible. He has not been a hidden scholar, content to see the result of his patient researches in print. He has come to the crowd of eager students with his treasures, and has displayed them with all the enthusiasm of an inveterate explorer.

I write, then, of no dry-as-dust theologian, whose conclusions may be studied, but whose personality is of little interest to the student. I write of one who all his life has arrested us not only by his teaching but by the way in which he has taught. We all know what it is to hear a clever expositor who, because he is a teacher only, leaves us cold. Dr. Morgan appeals to the brain. At the same time he warms the heart. He is the kind of schoolmaster we listen to and profit by because he is so exact, so careful, so sure of his ground, yet so thoroughly alive that he could not bore his students if he tried to.

Now you have probably heard of the man who proudly boasted, "I have gone through the Bible three times." "Ah," said a Minister quietly, "*has it ever gone through you once?*". Dr Morgan has taken us through the Bible. He has seen to it that it went through us. It has gone through him.

Of course he has been far more than a distinguished expositor. He has been an out-and-out evangelist. It is for his illuminating expositions of the Sacred Word that he will be best remembered. Some men are good preachers, but very poor teachers. They can rouse people, but having done that, with such gifts as God has given them, they leave it to others to train and educate them. Dr. Morgan has never been called "a popular evangelist". I do not think he would appreciate any such title. Had he not consecrated all his talents in the service of the Kingdom, one could imagine him as the Governor of a great College, or the Head of a Public School. He has been a kindly school-master, whose one subject is the Word of God. He has come to hundreds of thousands of students on both sides of the Atlantic as a reliable professor might come to a lecture room, not to tickle, or please, or amuse, not to play on the emotions but to *teach*.

When Dr. T. Wilkinson Riddle returned from America, he said he found everywhere outstanding preachers who confessed that they owed almost everything to Campbell Morgan. Among those named were Dr. J. D. Sandfer, the President of Hardin-Simmons University, Texas; Dr. M. E. Dodd, former President of the Southern Baptist Convention and Dr. M. E. Jenkens, of Abilene. Their whole career had been influenced. Dr. Dodd said: "He turned me from the popular topical method to pursue the expository method in my preaching." Dr. Ferrier Hulme has said: "Men and women in all parts of the world, and in all sections of

the Church of Christ, will tell you they owe
more than words can express to this bond-
servant of Jesus Christ. That is surely the
preacher's distinguished service medal. St. Paul
coveted no greater distinction, and was proud
of the designation."

I say Dr. Morgan has not been a " popular "
preacher in the sense in which that word has
been applied to some evangelists, to some
humorous or unconventional preachers, to some
polished orators. I think many years ago the
crowds that came to hear him surprised him.
Perhaps they do still. Those who will flock to a
preacher in order to sit at his feet as students
are not as those who are first attracted by a win-
some personality or a romantic story.

In quite recent years Dr. Morgan has conducted
special missions in many central Churches.
Like his friend, Dr. Norwood, who left the
City Temple feeling the call to such work, he
has recognised his limitations and kept to his
own particular line. I mean that he, like Dr.
Norwood again, has not been able to make any
special use of musical gifts, has not sought
particularly to appeal to the emotions of his
congregations in the service of song.

The doctor has always loved and admired a romantic personality like Gipsy Smith. Many and many a time he has been delighted to see how such an evangelist can sway a crowd. He himself has been here, as everywhere, the forceful *teacher*, with a clear-cut argument to be closely followed, cogent points to be remembered, Biblical quotations to be noted. I do not know that he has used decision cards, as Dr. Norwood has sometimes. There has always been intense force in his quiet, closing appeals. He preaches for a verdict. As he says in his book on Preaching, the closing note must be " *Thou art the man* ". That is the impression that must be left upon the hearer. " This man has not been preaching to the man next to me. He has been appealing to *my* intellect, to *my* emotion, to *my* will. I feel what he says is true of *me*."

Something more must be said of method later. With regard to Dr. Morgan himself (without any of that fulsome flattery which such a man must always detest), I think next of his glorious catholicity. You never think of him in con-nection with " ists " and " isms "; you do not look upon him as what has been called an *insect*arian.

To me it is always interesting to note that all through his career, and perhaps in a marked degree in these latter days, Dr. Morgan has gone out of his way to show his undying interest in and love for Methodism. The reasons for this are pretty well known, and I shall not enlarge upon them. His father, the Rev. George Morgan, was not a Methodist but a Baptist Minister, who eventually preferred to preach to an independent congregation. At Roath Road, Cardiff, young Morgan heard many famous Wesleyan preachers. His own first sermon was preached in the school-room of the Wesleyan Chapel at Monmouth, when he was thirteen. When he was twenty-five he was one of 150 candidates offering themselves for the Wesleyan Ministry. Of that number 105 were rejected, and Dr. Morgan was one of them.

That is an old story. I have heard many Methodist ministers apologising semi-humorously when they have been fraternising with Dr. Morgan at public meetings. As a matter of fact, nobody wishes that he had been accepted. God had a work for him to do. He might not long have remained in any Methodist Church. It was something like the unexpected change that came in the life of the Gipsy when he left the Salvation Army. Dr. Morgan entered the Congregational Ministry, but all along he has cultivated the friendship of Methodists. He proved, by the way, a true friend to the Rev. J. Gregory Mantle, who was one of the three ministers who had reported unfavourably on his trial sermon. I will not dwell on this—though I should like to. There have been preachers who could brilliantly pass all tests, win all academic distinctions, dazzle by their erudition : they have not always been able, away from the crowd, to exhibit the spirit of Christ, to stand by the very men against whom the petty soul might feel if not a grudge, at least some sort of prejudice.

The great preacher, Dr. Dale, of Birmingham, was very kind to Dr. Morgan in many ways. Once when the latter spoke rather dolefully of himself as " an untrained man ", Dr. Dale said a word he never forgot : " Don't say you are untrained. *Always remember God has many ways of training men.*" How true it is that " the beauty of Jesus " is quite independent of the Theological College classroom.

Certain it is that Dr. Morgan from his earliest

years felt the hand of God was guiding his every move. I have heard him tell the most illuminating story of the crisis of 1886, when, after a short period as teacher at the Wesleyan Day School at Islington, Birmingham, he was a master under Principal Levy in the Jewish Collegiate School. He felt all through his three years at this School that he must devote himself wholly to the work of preaching the Gospel, but decided that he dared not take this step because his parents were dependent upon him. The longing persisted in his heart and would not be silenced. One night he said to God : " If I am to go as Thy messenger, Thou wilt have to force me."

The very next morning the Principal told him that very shortly his services would have to be dispensed with, as the School was going to be closed. That was how God did force him out, and he became a Wesleyan Lay Evangelist.

Most readers will be aware that while Dr. Morgan has never written autobiographically, his biography up to eight or nine years ago was very ably written by the Rev. John Harries, of Marietta, Penva., and it is not my intention to repeat the interesting details he gave with regard to the doctor's American travels. " Have you lived here all your life?" they asked the oldest inhabitant, and he replied, " Not yet." I am thankful to say the complete account of Dr. Morgan's life cannot yet be written. In many such a career one is not able to say as one can say here, that the sunset is the most beautiful part of a glorious day. That will not be misunderstood. Many a great man has to give in before passing the allotted span because of his physical infirmities. As I write, Dr. Morgan is seventy-five, and in spite of many periods of weakness and suffering of one kind and another, he is preaching at the moment with extraordinary power.

I do not know that in a sketch of this kind, chronology matters very much, but what follows may be made clearer by bearing in mind a few stages in the journey :

1863 (Dec. 9th). Born at Tetbury, Gloucestershire.

1883–86. Master in the Jewish Collegiate School, Birmingham.

1886–88. Mission preacher.

1889.   Ordained to Congregational Ministry.

1889–91.   Pastorate at Stone, Staffs.

1891–93.   Pastorate at Rugeley, Staffs.

1893–97.   Westminster Road, Birmingham.

1897–1901. New Court Tollington Park, London.

1901–04.   Northfield Bible Conference Extension Lecturer.

1902.   Degree of Divinity conferred by the Chicago Theological Seminary.

1904–17.   First Ministry Westminster Chapel.

1911–14.   Principal of Cheshunt College.

1918.   Y.M.C.A. work at Mildmay.

1918–19.   Highbury Quadrant Congregational Church.

1919–29.   Bible Lectures, U.S.A.

1927–28.   Los Angeles Bible Institute.

1929–32.   Pastor of Tabernacle Presbyterian Church, Philadelphia, also Gordon College of Theology and Missions, Boston, etc.

1933.   Came back to help Dr. Simpson at Westminster.

1935.   Assumed once more full ministerial
responsibility at Westminster.

1936.   Diamond Jubilee as a preacher.

Happily at the time of writing one can add the word familiar to readers of newspaper reports— " *Proceeding !*"

CHAPTER II

Westminster Chapel—Its services—Its preachers—How
Dr. Morgan came to the pulpit—memories of D. L.
Moody—The War—Dr. Jowett—Dr. Morgan in America
—The Westminster Bible School.

CHAPTER II

When I think of the London preachers of thirty years ago, I always think of hidden little Bishopsgate Chapel, which has so many memories that I went the other day to gaze once more upon the altered scene. What great Nonconformist preacher in London did not appear in its pulpit at those hurried lunch hour services which good Thomas Grear made so popular? Dr. Morgan was there—with Dr. F. B. Meyer, Dr. Dinsdale Young, Dr. John Clifford, C. Silvester Horne, W. J. Dawson, Morgan Gibbon, Moffat Gautry, Luke Wiseman, S. W. Hughes, Charles Brown, R. C. Gillie—oh, I can't think of them all! Though the City Temple has had weekday services at times since, and Wesley's Chapel has them now, there has never been anything quite like the interdenominational character of these long-continued services arranged by Thomas Grear, at which preachers had so skilfully to exercise the art of condensation.

It is a great temptation to compare those pre-war days with these, I will resist it.

Great as has been his work in America, we shall always think of Dr. Morgan as " of Westminster Chapel ". It is possible that some who read this have never seen this famous Congregational Church. It has seen great Ministries, and the striking bust of Samuel Martin which is the first thing you see as you enter reminds you of the first of them. It will always be pre-eminently associated with the name of Dr. Morgan. Outside, you may see at the right hand corner a stone with a longish inscription which gives some information about the building. The first Chapel on the site of the old Westminster Hospital, was built in 1840, and Samuel Martin was the first Minister. Schools and institutional premises were soon added, but became wholly inadequate, and the present Chapel was erected in 1864, when Mr. Martin was still the Minister.

It is not as large as the Metropolitan Tabernacle, but it is, next to that wonderful building, perhaps the most striking Nonconformist Church in London, with its air of spaciousness, and its two big galleries. Many in the congregations must have come long distances. I should not describe the company gathered here as of the kind you would expect to see in a great Mission

Hall. It is one composed mostly of those whom we call middle-class people, professional men, city men, young students. They give one the impression that they have not only come to worship, but that the sermon is a very important thing indeed ; they have come to be *taught*. Open Bibles are seen in almost every pew. Many of the young people take notes. They love the way in which this man teaches them. " Let us imagine we are in the Primary Department with Miss ——," I heard him say one night when he was putting things with great simplicity. They smiled. They knew Miss —— and they knew they were children in school, after all.

Often I used to walk on a Sunday from North London to Buckingham Gate, passing towards the end of the journey, those dark, precipitous mansions, which were then London's only sky scrapers, before the gigantic Transport House made its appearance almost opposite. I went, like everybody else, to worship—and to learn. So far as I know, Westminster Chapel has never been talked of to any great extent because of its musical performances, its choir festivals, and so forth. People have not flocked there because there was anything sensational in a musical way.

The Chapel has a very fine organ which one has always liked to hear, and for many a year Mr. E. Emlyn Davies, F.R.C.O., has played it with unobtrusive skill, using all his talents to help the preacher and the true spirit of Worship. The Choir is not conspicuous ; it is not gowned ; but it is efficient. It is not a help, but a hindrance, when in any church the organ is overpowering, and the choir has too much of a monopoly. It is such a relief sometimes to come to a great church like this and find the family are content audibly to repeat the Lord's Prayer together, instead of lazily leaving the choir to sing it. Dr. Morgan may not claim to have great musical gifts, but he has very keen musical appreciation, and he does know quite surely what kind of music he wants at Westminster. The congregational singing strikes one as being excellent. It is never boisterous, but it is at least intelligent ; and all the more helpful because tunes as well as the words are familiar, and there are not too many risky experiments.

One will never forget the days in which Dr. Morgan first ministered at Westminster Chapel. Congregationalism in London had some most remarkable men : Silvester Horne, R. F. Horton,

J. Morgan Gibbon, W. J. Dawson, Bernard
Snell, R. J. Campbell, and many others. Westminster Chapel, which has truly had its ups and
downs and its seasons of anxiety, had then
reached such a low ebb that it was well nigh
empty and bankrupt. I do not know how many
prominent preachers had declined its pulpit.
It may be imagined how applause burst out and
the Doxology was sung on the memorable day
on which Dr. Morgan first gave his decision to
accept the pastorate.

It is a great story. In 1896 the doctor had had
his first meeting with D. L. Moody. His great
friend, the Rev. Albert Swift, afterwards of East
Dulwich, but then in New York, arranged the
introduction, and Mr. Moody at once invited
the London preacher to give a series of Bible
Readings to his students at Chicago. At Methodist camp meetings and at the Northfield Summer
School the English visitor became known to
ever-growing audiences. " Campbell Morgan,"
Mr. Moody said, " is the most remarkable man
I have ever had at Northfield."

And what did Dr. Morgan say of Moody ?
When the great evangelist died, Dr. Morgan sent
to his son a tribute in which he said :

" My personal acquaintance with D. L. Moody was not of long duration, according to the measure of the calendar. If, however, we should count time by heart throbs, I may claim to have known him, for it was one of the greatest privileges of my life to come very near to him in the ripest years of his life. I first saw him in 1883 during his second visit to Birmingham. Bingley Hall was being crowded with eager multitudes who had come by train from the whole surrounding districts. Once only I spoke to him. I remember no detail of arrangement escaped his notice. A vacant seat, the opening and closing of doors, a tendency to drag the singing—all these he noted and rectified.

" I did not see him again for thirteen years, but through them all the force of his character had an influence upon my life that I should find it hard to measure. In 1896 I visited the United States for the first time. The Northfield Conference was in session, and I managed to spend a few hours there. It was a field day for me, as well as a revelation ! Everywhere Mr. Moody was the moving spirit. Bright, cheery, and yet in dead earnest, he seemed to make everything go before him.

" In the intervals of the meeting he gave me a drive round the campus in his buggy. Every point of interest was pointed out, and in a few brief words, the story of how the different buildings were erected was told. Suddenly he pulled up his horse to speak to a group of children and to tell them to go to his house and get all the apples they wanted. He drove through a gate to where a man was at work in a field. 'Bylow,' he said, ' it's too hot for you to work much. Half a day's work for a day's pay while this heat lasts.' I sat by his side and watched, and began to understand the greatness of the man whose life was so broad that it touched sympathetically all other phases of life.

" When after the evening meeting I gathered with the speakers at his house for the first time, I saw him in a new rôle, that of the host. He sat in a chair at the head of the table, directed the conversation, and listened with the patience and simplicity of a child to every word the others spoke. As we departed, I went to bid him good-bye as I was to leave by an early train on the morrow. 'Oh,' he said, 'I shall see you : you are to preach at ten o'clock. That was the first intimation I had of it. It was his way. I did preach as he had bid me, as other and better men had been glad to do. After speaking next morning I hurried away, but in that brief stay Moody had become more to me—strong, tender, considerate. From that day I more than revered him: I loved him."

Some details of the work Dr. Morgan did in America year after year will be found in Mr. Harries' "Life". I must refer to one story which I have heard the doctor tell of his acceptance of the Westminster Pastorate in 1903.

"I came home," he said, "for a visit. I preached at Westminster. I was asked to accept the pastorate. I was committed to America for Conferences that would last at least a year. The little band of men who had held the fort at Westminster against a great deal of misunderstanding asked me to reconsider the matter in a year. I said I would, if they promised in the meantime if anyone else appeared, they would not hesitate to call him.

"In that year someone else did appear, Dr. Smith, of St. Paul and Minneapolis, and they invited him. He, however, did not see his way to accept, and I came back in 1904 to look over the ground and consider the opportunity which

Westminster offered. I felt at once the building was a great preaching auditorium than which none is more acoustically perfect.

"I preached through the month of June, having promised to give answer to the invitation on the third Sunday. On the morning of that day I was staying in Dulwich with Albert Swift.

"My father was there. When I came down to breakfast early, he said, ' What are you going to do ?'

"I replied, ' I don't know.'

"After a hasty breakfast, I went up to my room and got down on my knees alone, and said, ' Master, what shall I do ?'

"I heard no voice replying, but I had an answer as clearly and distinctly and directly as any man ever had a word from God, and this was the answer : ' Make your own choice. I am with you, whether in the States or in London.

"It was a new experience in my spiritual life to feel I was flung back upon my own choosing, and I said to myself, How shall I choose ? There came to me at once the familiar but great statement, ' The just shall live by faith.'

"At once I felt the matter was settled.

"In a certain sense, faith was not necessary if I went back to America. For instance, John Wannamaker had told me if I would stay he was prepared to put up a Bible School and Institute of which I should have charge, with an assured salary. Moreover, my arrangements with the Northfield Conferences was a settled one, as to finance. On this side nothing was arranged. The Church had no endowments. Here was the place where the activity of faith would be necessary.

"I chose on that principle."

Dr. Wilkinson Riddle, who was present at Dr. Morgan's induction at Westminster Chapel in November, 1904, when Dr. J. H. Jowett preached a memorable sermon on the two words "Destructive Heresies", records that Dr. A. E. Garvie had described Westminster Chapel as a "white elephant"—a statement which gave the new minister an opportunity of proving that white elephants were very sacred, rare and wonderful creatures!

Certain it is that Dr. Morgan and his great friend and colleague, Mr. Swift turned the despair of Congregationalism into a success. Establishing a strong Church life, and work

among the young, their outstanding achievement
was the founding of the Bible School (to which
I will make further reference) with an average
attendance of eighteen hundred, gathered each
Friday night from all parts of London, and the
surrounding country. I remember how when the
Great War broke out Westminster Chapel was
crowded to excess. People sat on window ledges,
rostrum steps, on extra chairs. Miss Jane T.
Stoddart has truly said that Dr. Morgan rose
to his greatest heights as a preacher on the
August Sunday of 1914 before and after the
declaration of war. Invaluable service was
rendered by him at that time to the people of
London, to the nation, and to the Allied Cause.

During the War—in 1917—the doctor rendered valuable service to the Y.M.C.A. by giving
lectures at Mildmay to men who were going to
France. Then for a year he preached at Highbury
Quadrant Congregational Church, that fine building in which one had so often heard Dr. W. J.
Dawson before he went to America. Dr. Morgan
was unsettled about this time (how few of us
were not !), and his health peremptorily demanded
a change of climate. He therefore accepted some
of the countless invitations that came to him

for Bible Conference work in different parts of the United States.

Here some reference must be made to that silver-tongued preacher with whose name, also, Westminster Chapel must ever be associated— Dr. John Henry Jowett. It will be remembered that when he closed his great ministry in Carr's Lane, Birmingham, he went to Fifth Avenue Presbyterian Church, New York, in 1911.

Dr. Jowett always had an idea that he would end his days as minister of the City Temple, but it was not to be.

He quite plainly hinted that a home call would be welcomed by him, and when Dr. Morgan closed his first pastorate at Westminster in 1917, within a month a special Church meeting had invited him to the pulpit. I believe when he came to the Chapel in the back streets between Victoria Street and St. James's Park he was not at all attracted by the building itself. " A Charing Cross Station of a Chapel," someone called it, and Dr. Jowett said the people in the galleries " seemed to belong to another planet ". He came, however, to a fine Evangelical atmosphere of a busy institutional premises built up in twelve years by Dr. Morgan.

Dr. Jowett said of his friend : " I never can decide whether Morgan's greater opportunity lies in a settled pastorate, or in a wider ministry in many lands." America has held out great attractions for some of our most beloved preachers —and we have sometimes honestly grudged their going there. Of course we have realised that they were using great opportunities. There was quite an outcry when Dr. Morgan left for the States in 1919. Perhaps some were a little too emphatic in their protests. It is not for us to decide these things. I can imagine a preacher saying, " I can extend my sphere of influence. God is calling me to people who can appreciate my message. I have been feeling the strain of pouring out my soul week after week to the great London congregation. I can cover so much more ground on the other side of the Atlantic ; I can reach so many more people. At the same time, I can use some of the material which I have so carefully prepared and given here, and that will mean an opportunity for a much-needed rest." There are several distinguished preachers who have exercised their ministry on both sides of the herring-pond. Incidentally, they have helped to strengthen the bonds of friendship and sympathy between the two great peoples.

Anyway, Dr. Jowett came from America, and preached magnificently at Westminster until his health failed and he had to retire, shortly before his death in 1923.

Then came the pastorate of Dr. John Hutton until 1925, when the Scottish preacher, so widely beloved, became the editor of the *British Weekly*. From 1928 to 1933 the pulpit was occupied by that much-travelled and warmly evangelistic scholar and preacher, Dr. Hubert Louis Simpson, whom one had first known in the Westbourne Church, Glasgow, where he ministered for so many years.

Meanwhile year after year, Dr. Morgan, who says no one may even realise what it cost him to lay down his work at Westminster and go out once more by faith, travelled up and down and across the United States and Canada, everywhere addressing large audiences, and arousing great interest in the study of the Word of God. He preached and lectured in nearly every state of the Union, and in all the Canadian provinces.

There followed a period of two and a half years, with Los Angeles Bible Institute as a base, from which centre he travelled up and down the Pacific coast, speaking at many centres within reach of Los Angeles. He then returned East in 1929 to take the pastorate of the Tabernacle Presbyterian Church in Philadelphia, where three happy years were spent. Also during that time for two years, he went to the Gordon College of Theology and Missions in Boston, Mass., for two days each week, to lecture to the students.

"Give me that grey, misty, cloudy island England, first and last," wrote J. H. Jowett when he was rather homesick in America. I fancy Dr. Morgan at times felt that way. Anyway in 1933 he was again at Westminster, helping Dr. Simpson, and in 1935 he settled down in the famous Chapel once more.

While writing of the Chapel, I must refer again to a feature of Dr. Morgan's first Ministry there, made still more notable in his second—the Bible School, which has gone from strength to strength in recent years. Out of this sprang the Bible Teachers' Association, which sent out so many young missionaries. This is not the place in which to deal with the far-spreading influence of the Mundesley Conference, which Dr. Morgan established in 1906, but I may say in parenthesis that hundreds will be looking back with gratitude to the holy-days spent in that quiet, health-giving little place. Dr. Morgan realised at least to some extent his dream of an English Northfield, and in five or six years the number of visitors attending became so great that accommodation was overtaxed. The official reports of the addresses given were published, and were of great value. It was with very deep regret that owing to war restrictions, his own bad health, and other reasons, Dr. Morgan had to give up the Mundesley meetings. There were, however, subsequent Conferences of the same kind, and those who attended them will never forget their influence.

Meanwhile, the Bible School has gone on to the present day with wonderful success and blessing. More than thirty years ago it was much as it is now. The Rev. Charles T. Cook, the Editor of *The Christian*, who first went to the School in 1904, says :

" That visit was a revelation. The lecture was on ' Christ and the Bible ', the third of several studies introductory to an analytical survey of the books of the New Testament. I was gripped instantly. It was not so much that the teaching was new—several of the arguments were already familiar to me—but there was something exceptionally arresting and dynamical about the preacher and his style.

" Thereafter, for three years, I do not think I missed a single lecture. A break then came owing to absence from London, but on my return to the Metropolis, I was back in my accustomed place. By this time I was a student in a theological college, and the Westminster Bible School meant more to me than ever.

" My debt to Dr. Morgan and his Bible School is beyond computation. I owe much to other men of God, but no man has done more to mould my life and service than Dr. Morgan. He it was who really opened my eyes to the value of systematic Bible study and Bible teaching. My resolve to make my own ministry centre in the exposition of the Word was due almost entirely to his influence.

" Like many another, I have often asked myself what is the secret of Dr. Morgan's pre-eminence and popularity as a Bible teacher? If I had to give it in one word, I think I should choose the term ' dynamic '. But what are the factors which impart that distinguishing quality to his ministry ? He loves the word ' teacher ';

but his lectures are far removed from the purely didactic. Teaching which is merely teaching may inform, but it does not inspire. And, let us make no mistake, the crowds flock to Westminster because first and foremost they find inspiration there. I agree, therefore, with the late Mrs. Herman in the opinion that Dr. Morgan is a great teacher because he is a born *preacher*.

"I had never properly understood how each book of the Bible has its own particular theme until Dr. Morgan revealed the fact by means of those compelling blackboard analyses thirty years ago. (I wish the present generation could have seen Dr. Morgan's skill with that blackboard !)

"His aim always is to let the Bible deliver its own message, and I know of no one who has demonstrated more convincingly the marvellous unity of the Divine Library. Large areas of Scripture, sadly neglected even by orthodox preachers, have been compelled to yield up rich treasures of truth. Any section he touches, begins to speak at once with living voice to our own generation."

When, just before writing this, I went to the Bible School, on a bitterly cold winter's night,

it was somewhat a surprise to me to find a
congregation which seemed to be even larger
than that of the Sunday evening. Surely there
was no more remarkable sight in the religious
life of London than such a crowd, gathered for
a solemn service, lasting not a minute beyond the
hour, very much like that of the Sabbath Day.
The people had come long distances—subur-
banites, Salvation Army soldiers, nurses, Sunday
School workers, ministers, all sorts and con-
ditions. The thing that struck me most was
their intense quietude. No restlessness, no
coughing, not a sound or movement ; all were
so anxious to catch every word—and the doctor,
who that night had come from his bed to lecture,
could not speak very loudly. On this occasion
the doctor was talking about the power of Jesus
over death, and of the figure of sleep, so common
in literature. With a little gleam of humour
he said he was not going into the subject of
dreams : he meant " normal, proper sleep you
have if you have had the right kind of supper ".
One of the most beautiful things about this
service was the singing, which I do not think I
had ever heard before, of " Sleep on beloved,
sleep and take thy rest. . . . Goodnight, Good-

night, goodnight." We were singing from the excellent hymn book, the Song Companion to the Scriptures, compiled by Dr. Morgan, and he read out a note in the music edition explaining that the early Christians were accustomed to bid their dying friends goodnight, so sure were they of their awakening on the Resurrection Morn. (I believe I am correct in saying that his father was fond of that hymn.)

There was nothing gruesome or morbid about the treatment of such a subject. We all went away with beautiful thoughts about the sleep of our beloved dead. And in the middle of the service we were told that the Bible School might look forward to a new series of lectures beginning in April and occupying three months! In con-nection with the celebration of the 400th anni-versary of the putting of the Bible in the Churches and making it available to the people, the doctor felt he must talk on " The Bible : Some con-structive reconsiderations ". In dealing with topics like the Romance of the Bible, the Unity of the Bible, the Authority of the Bible, the Bible and the Nation, the Bible and the Child, and so on, he would be covering old ground : some of it dealt with in books which I have mentioned.

In addition, there would be a great amount of
entirely new material.

Dr. Morgan has been, it goes without saying,
a lifelong supporter of The British and Foreign
Bible Society, of which he is a Vice-President.
The last time he addressed the Society's Annual
Meeting was, I think, in 1908, on which occasion
he created a deep impression. He said he would
put absolutely on one side the speech he had
prepared, and devote his time to fulfilling the
old-fashioned office of the Methodist Church,
that of the " Exhorter ".

" We are face to face with an awful indifference
to religion," said Dr. Morgan. " That is due to
the passionless condition of the Christian Church,
and that in turn is due to the utter uncertainty
of Christian people about the authority of the
Book of God. Suffer a word of personal conviction. Where is the remedy ? It is not by the
defence of the Word of God, but by its study
and by our own return to it until it so consumes
us that we shall be able to say, ' O Lord, how
I love thy law : it is my meditation day and
night.'

" I have no panic in my heart as to its ultimate
victory, my panic at the moment, if there is one

there, is for the men and women who are neg-
lecting it. My appeal is for a new devotion to
it, a new answer to it. When our own people,
of whatever section of the great catholic Church
of Christ, turn from books concerning it to the
Book itself, to know it, to understand it, to live
in the power of it, then you will have generated
within their hearts the passion which it teaches,
and for ever more makes possible to send the
same message on to those in darkness."

Mention must be made, too, of Dr. Morgan's
support of the International Bible Reading
Association. At one of the annual meetings of
the Association Dr. Morgan, as he often did,
modestly and almost apologetically added to
other speeches an "exhortation", with the
inevitably firstly, secondly, thirdly and fourthly.

"As a perpetual necessity to the reading of
the Bible," he said, "while there are many
methods, the one method which perhaps has
become almost a fanaticism with me is not the
only one, the first necessity is *Inspiration* : I do
not now mean belief in the inspiration of the
Bible. I want to insist that the Scriptures can
only be read intelligently by inspired men and
inspired women and inspired children. The

value we get from our daily reading will be in proportion to the measure in which we are filled with the Spirit of God.

" *The next thing is Breadth.* I do not want to introduce a note of controversy, but I have felt for a long time that on some of those very rare occasions when the International lesson fixed has been a very difficult one to deal with, that difficulty has been again and again redeemed by the grouping round it of passages of Scripture. I have been amazed at the skill with which the work is done. I always read that portion aloud at the family altar in my own home and read it with great interest. A breadth of outlook is necessary for the study of the Bible and that breadth is perpetually supplied by the skill with which these passages are grouped.

" Then there must be *Regularity* in the study of the Scripture. We have to face the fact that the family altar has broken down. It is appalling that you should find so many Christian homes in which there is no family altar. It is a commonplace to say that we can no more live the spiritual life without perpetual and regular study of the Word than we can live our physical life without proper sustenance."

"I was brought up," said Dr. Morgan, "in one of those homes where the simple blunt rule concerning the family altar was this. If under any circumstances it was necessary that either the breakfast or the family altar should be forfeited, it was the breakfast that had to go. If we could only make that the rule of our lives I venture to say that the breakfast would very seldom be missed.

"The last thing I am now thinking of as necessary," he added, "is an *application* of the Scripture as we come to hear it in our daily life. We are to take our daily reading and carry it with us to the store, to the office, to school, wherever we go, assimilating it for the strengthening of our own spiritual life, but applying it so that the world may be made the sweeter and the better."

I cannot stay to refer to the many branches of work carried on on the Westminster Chapel's premises, as I am dealing with a man, and not with organisations; but all who know the Chapel know how ably its multifarious work is planned and carried out week by week, and how invaluable through the years has been the quiet, efficient work of Dr. Morgan's colleague and right-hand man, Mr. Arthur Marsh, than whom no one living could present a true portrait of a beloved chief. I ought to add that Westminster Chapel would be badly off without its admirably edited *Record*, which has passed on so many of Dr. Morgan's sermons and Bible lectures. No Church could have a magazine of greater value. Among the many and varied activities of the Westminster Church the bookroom and library are very keenly appreciated.

CHAPTER III

Pen Portraits—Dr. Morgan in the pulpit—Tributes from his friends—Dr. Morgan and the children.

CHAPTER III

It is a little difficult to avoid some description of
Dr. Morgan's personal appearance. I have seen
many attempts, of the kind which must be very
distasteful to the subject. Perhaps if he has a
sense of humour he consoles himself with the
reflection that when a man is distinguished by
what he has done people must needs want to
know how he looks. I suppose it has always
been considered to be an honour to be caricatured
in *Punch*.

I dislike as much as you do empty talk of a
preacher's "handsome presence", "charming
smile", and all that sort of thing. Those personal
details matter so little. If you never saw Dr.
Morgan, let this suffice. He was always a striking
figure—tall, thin, wiry, with a shock of wavy
hair, quite dark when first I saw it, now (1938)
snow white; a lean, rather drawn countenance,
in profile reminding one sometimes of a certain
picture of a dignified Egyptian Monarch. There
was one other great preacher, much loved in
America and at one time well known here, who

had some resemblance to Dr. Morgan. I refer to Dr. Len. G. Broughton of Atlanta. Several times I saw them standing side by side and thought they might have been brothers—as, in everything but birth, indeed they were.

No ! Dr. Morgan is not one of those preachers with regard to whom we make stupid remarks about personal magnetism, attractive presence, charming delivery, and so on and so forth. Little he cares about that sort of thing. The people who have flocked to hear him everywhere have gone because of his message. I know what he says counts because of what he *is*. These people as anyone could tell on studying the Westminster congregation for a minute, come, as I have been insisting, because they want to be *taught*. I have seen quite a number of them making notes in little books as he preached, as if in class ; and that is a much easier thing to do in the case of a preacher who sets out his points so clearly and concisely.

An American journalist once compared his " stance " at the reading desk with that of Abraham Lincoln in his great orations. Another contrasted his personal appearance with Mr. Moody's. " The elder man was tall and broad-

chested, and Mr. Morgan is very thin. His clothes
hang loosely on his body. His features are sharp.
His eyes burn like coals of fire beneath over-
hanging eyebrows. He is a man who would
impress one at a first glance." And so on ; I will
not quote more. Some writers have said he was
like George Eliot, some that he was like Henry
Irving. He is like neither. Another picturesque
journalist said he " could have passed for Augus-
tine in his old age, Pope Gregory, a Spanish
Grand Inquisitor, an Archbishop of York or
Canterbury ". I know well enough that these
are trivialities. Unlike some of his friends in the
Congregational Ministry, the doctor always has
the look of a Minister. You cannot mistake his
calling. Say what you will in the argument for
and against clerical uniform, far too many men
of God are slovenly in their dress to-day. The
wearing of a gown in the pulpit is not a matter of
vital importance. At the same time I think a
great deal might be said of the remarkable
opportunities for service to God that have come
to men who have not hesitated in their everyday
dress to proclaim their sacred calling. Sometimes
I hear a Minister say laughingly, " The man
talked on, having no idea that I was a parson."

That is nothing to boast about. The man ought to have made the discovery in two minutes.

I do not suppose that at any period of his life Dr. Morgan has been physically robust. When he was a lad of seven or eight his life was despaired of, indeed there was one day during an attack of pneumonia when he was actually thought to be dead. I marvel at the record of the strenuous days he spent as a young minister in London. The pace would seem to have been killing, with calls for missions, lectures, addresses, not only in the Metropolis, but all over the country. Yet he was not allowed to kill himself, even if at times he seemed to come perilously near it. His friends know that time after time, even if he has defied his doctors, he has recognised and obeyed the guiding hand of God.

The doctor must forgive me if I ask leave to quote from one vivid account of a visit to Westminster Chapel which appeared in a series of rather brilliant articles by " Eutychus " in *Truth*.

" It was," said the writer, " a Bible Divine at the Westminster Congregational Church, who plays upon texts as if they were so many stops

of an organ." After a description of the church
the article proceeded :

" The congregation strikes a friendly note.
Those with hymn-books provide for those without." (I do not think this can often be necessary,
as one is given a book on entering). " Sunday
morning provides a generous supply of lavender
water upon clean handkerchiefs. Those with
coughs carry polite lozenges. There is no un-
seemly scrambling for seats. Five minutes before
the hour, which is in your interests (the sidesman
has been giving frequent glances at his watch),
the seatholders' rights lapse, and he beckons one
candidate for a seat, then the next, and places
them."

" Eutychus " described Dr. Morgan thus :
"A magnificent figure in his black gown with
velvet strappings, and the crimson hood which
catches him across the throat. He has an aloofness
and is full of dignity and withal an eye which
penetrates here, penetrates there and is not in-
different to his congregation. The eyebrows
make a circumflex. They are prominent, over-
hanging the deepset eyes. They work as the
preacher is moved, now here, now there. The
long gaunt face . . . a face of hard experience.

A temperamental face, not unlike that of an old
prophet; not ascetic, but tense: acutely sus-
ceptible to life. Alive to the last breath. Muscles
always tightening from ear to chin, holding
the head back, lending it a dominant lift. Hair
is dead white, but vigorous, that no brushing
could make meek. No stiffness when he speaks
—mobility, will power.

"A head master, rather awe-inspiring. His
voice is well cadenced belonging to an era of
oratory that is past and that included Dickens
among its members. He reads in short phrases
with an emphasis on the last word, sometimes
singing the last word."

The writer, having quoted from the sermon,
concluded: "Here is a man who knows his
Bible inside out, whose fresh and vivid use of
words can make an old truth new and explain
the hold to-day upon a British congregation of
the Scriptures of an obscure tribe of long ago
and far away."

On the whole, that may seem to be a pretty
fair impression from a broad-minded journalist
who was visiting many churches and hearing
many voices.

But enough of pen portraits. They are rarely

satisfactory. Dr. Morgan looks like the scholar he is. I do not think political life would have suited him. He might have been a great medical man. One thing is certain. In his youth no one who knew him would ever have prophesied for him any career that did not involve hard study and concentrated thought.

The Rev. Albert Swift, writing of his closest friend, once said : " Most strangers probably feel that there is at first a certain shyness and reserve about him, but as a matter of fact, he is a most genial and cordial man. To enjoy his friendship means the enriching of one's life. No service he can give is of too great a cost, whilst his love combines the strength of a noble man with the tenderness of a gentle woman. The dominant note of his ministry is the will of God, and I believe that the one desire of his heart is to ever live and work within the compass of that brief but comprehensive prayer, ' Thy will be done.' "

In a revealing and intimate talk to his people, Dr. Morgan himself said : " I don't think my friends would describe me as unsociable, but I cannot bear near me anybody who creates in me a feeling of restraint. I am slow to make friends, or to talk to strangers. What would suit me would be a house buried in the woods, a quick transit to a crowded church—and back to the woods!"

He would say that with a smile. One can understand it so well. Of all people, I am sure his friend Dr. Jowett would have understood it. He, too, had a certain shy reserve. He hated the familiar stranger who plunges into an undesired conversation. All preachers know well how, especially in times of strain when they are concentrating on their message, they dislike foolish aimless chatter that has no depth at all.

But Dr. Morgan has been far more genial than some who did not know him have imagined. His sons can tell many a story of how when his life was most strenuous he was always their playmate, ready to take part in any game, from marbles to cricket and lawn tennis, in which they were interested. In earlier years his strength and agility astonished them. I remember a friend saying of the late Dr. Jowett that he would have had a longer life if he had taken part in games when a young man. Dr. Morgan has been blessed with four lads, and they saw to it that their father did not get rusty!

Not a few notable preachers in the Christian Church, by the way, can claim to be sons of the manse, but it is given to very few ministers of Christ to have four sons, each of whom has devoted his life to the service of the Gospel. It is not surprising that this fact has been an occasion of the greatest joy to both Dr. and Mrs. Morgan. As an indication of the spiritual freedom of this entirely united household, it is interesting to note that the four sons have chosen their own pathway from a denominational point of view.

Percival, although reared as a Congregationalist, felt led to seek Confirmation and to join the Church of England. After a curacy in North-East London, Mr. Percival Campbell Morgan became Curate at St. John's Church, Hove, where his preaching was greatly appreciated by large numbers of visitors. A few months ago, however, he received Preferment and was made Vicar of St. James's Church, Brighton. This church, which is situated in a working-class neighbourhood, offers immense scope for that type of work on which Mr. Percival Morgan's heart is set.

Another son, Howard Moody, has the unique

distinction of having succeeded his father as Minister of the Tabernacle Presbyterian Church in Philadelphia. Of recent summers Howard Moody has paid a visit to Great Britain and has occupied with much acceptance the pulpits of the City Temple and of College Road, Harrow.

A third son, Kingsley John, is also doing valuable work in a city church in Louisville, Kentucky, U.S.A.

I have left to the last Frank Crossley Morgan, because, in the mind of those most competent to judge, he more nearly resembles his father than the other three. In the summer of 1935 during Dr. Morgan's breakdown in health, he took his father's place at the Westminster Bible School. Dr. Morgan was quite confident that for a week or two the kind friends at Westminster would take his boy to their heart, if only for his sake; but, he confesses that he would not have been surprised had the interest diminished after the first two or three lectures. To his great joy and satisfaction, however, the numbers increased steadily, and on every hand there were sympathetic words of appreciation of the young preacher's firm grasp of the Scriptures of truth.

Dr. Crossley Morgan has felt led to give up the pastorate of the Presbyterian Church in Augusta, Georgia, in order that he may devote himself to the wider ministry of preaching and Bible lecturing. In this way, history continues to repeat itself, and Christian people on the American continent are lavish in their praise and appreciation of one who so worthily is following in his father's footsteps.

Of the two daughters, one has chosen to remain by the side of her mother and father, and for many years has been a source of comfort and strength to them both. The other is happily married to a London business man, and both he and his wife have found a spiritual home at Westminster.

I have introduced this little fragment of family history in order to show that Dr. Morgan's influence begins at Jerusalem, even though it does not end there. A cynical Frenchman once said that " No man could be a hero to his own valet ". Dr. Morgan has gone one better; he is a hero to his own children.

I do not think railway travelling has ever tired him much. Like other preachers, he has had real rest when crossing the Atlantic in good weather, for the deck has been the one place where he has not had the regular hours of a study. He used to play golf a good deal. When at Northfield he loved to drive out in the beautiful Connecticut Valley. One of the most sacred spots in the world to him has been D. L. Moody's last resting place on Round Top.

There is no reference to the doctor's " recreations " in *Who's Who*, but in earlier years he was no stranger to healthy athletics. When a lad at the Douglas Private School at Cheltenham, Principal Butler made him play cricket, and he says though he could not bat very well he was not bad at bowling (many years later he sent his own sons to this School). When he was a schoolmaster in Birmingham his Principal, who had at one time been an amateur weight-lifting champion of Britain, described him as a very good bowler, who captained the boys' team in all their matches. The boys loved him because he so heartily joined in their sports.

When I have seen and heard Dr. Morgan in recent days, I could not help thinking how well he has learned to grow old gracefully. He seemed to me to have mellowed, to have become more tender in his tones, more generous in his outlook —not less sure, but more so ; yet, dare I say, more gentle in his assurance. I do like the story of the Minister grown old in the service who could not speak loudly enough to be heard by half the congregation. He offered to resign, and his people would not hear of it. One of them said, " Why, it's a sermon just to see the dear old doctor walk into the pulpit. His very presence is a blessing and a benediction !"

Happily at the moment Dr. Morgan is able to do the work he loves ; but I have noted one or two occasions on which his presence, even in silence, brought a message.

I do not think he has ever cared a rap about newspaper publicity. When his Jubilee was celebrated recently, the newspaper men did not fire questions at him as they did in the cases of Dinsdale Young and Gipsy Smith. I know what he did want. Some years ago he said : " I crave to-day more than I ever did in my life with a greater longing than I ever felt to know that men and women are praying for me. In New York three men came and looked into my face and said : ' For five years we three have prayed for you every day by solemn covenant.' I cannot tell you what it meant to me."

His old friend, Dr. Ferrier Hulme, had the great privilege of staying in his home at Glendale, California, in 1928. " Many hundreds of students there," he says, " will ever remember with gratitude his remarkable work as the Biblical Professor at what was known as BIOLA—the Bible Institute of Los Angeles. I saw the grip he had on their minds and hearts, and how he stimulated their mental alertness. At Riverside also, several miles away in one of the loveliest spots on God's earth, his hearers were wont to hang on his lips, as, like his Master, ' he opened to them the Scriptures '.

" The same applies to other centres in the Far West ; but the deepest impression of all produced on my wife and self was in his own well-ordered home. Family prayer there was a rare delight, and a real means of grace. His reverent reading of the Word, the voices of his household as they sang so sweetly some selection from the songs of the saints of all ages, with one of his daughters at the piano, and the fervent petitions that followed in choice phraseology."

" My wife and I," said Dr. Hulme, " stayed with him again at Philadelphia, in the manse adjoining the Presbyterian Church of which he was then pastor, and where his son Howard has been exercising such a fruitful ministry. My bedroom adjoined Dr. Morgan's study. If I am not an early riser, I am an early waker, and I used to notice at 5.30 in the morning between the chinks of the door that the study lights were on. I soon found that this great expositor was morning by morning at his desk enriching his own mind and heart with the treasures of the Sacred Book."

That reminds me that in 1938 Dr. Morgan was forbidden by his doctor to preach more than once on Sunday. The Sunday after his friend and neighbour, Dr. Dinsdale Young, died, he did a beautiful thing. He had preached at Westminster Chapel in the morning. In the evening he unexpectedly arrived and took part in the service at the Westminster Central Hall. I shall never forget that service because a moving sermon was preached by Dr. Ferrier Hulme at the age of 82. Dr. Young had died at the age of 76. Dr. Morgan who came to bring the sympathy of his congregation, was 75 !

Dr. T. Wilkinson Riddle, F.R.S.L., formerly of Plymouth, describes Dr. Morgan as " in turn the idol of my youth, the despair of my middle thirties, and the joy of my early fifties !" He has long regarded the doctor as a preacher without a rival.

Dr. Riddle has thus summed up his friend's great qualities :

" First, friendship. Sometimes people have spoken to me about his aloofness : but that is only the price of his staunchness. He realises with Emerson that friendships are costly. Once he takes you to his heart, you are grappled to him with hooks of steel. Through fair weather and foul weather, you may rely on him. He will never let you down.

" Second, amazing charity. I am not thinking so much of financial benevolence, although he has done more of that than most people I know. I am thinking, rather, of his generous estimate even of those who have made somewhat of a mess of things. He is swift to praise, and slow to blame. More than once we have discussed a man whose life has ended in such an eclipse that not even a corona was left. And all he has said has been : ' Poor chap.'

"Finally, his generosity. I have never known a man less conceited. His heart swells, but not his head. I have proved him not only to be a great encourager, but one who lavished almost extravagant praise upon another's efforts."

I have never seen much of Dr. Morgan among the children. Most of us know him best as the teacher of grown-up children who are never too old to learn. He was President of the Sunday School Union over thirty years ago. He was not called to do any special work among the little ones, but those who saw him in his own home when his boys were with him knew how fully he could enter into the fun and frolic of childhood. With all his natural gravity when dealing with profound themes, in the pulpit he has been, except in the too frequent periods of strain and ill-health, youthful in his outlook.

He has always loved to recall the old days in the nursery at Roath, Cardiff, where at the age of seven he conducted such solemn services preaching to his beloved little sister (who went to Heaven two years later) and a congregation of dolls. Many a time have we heard and read of great preachers who gave promise in a nursery

of the career to which they were to be called :
I do not think I know of one who has looked
back with such tenderness as Dr. Morgan does
upon the little draped pulpit in the nursery
and the dear little girl who so gravely
brought her " family " to hear the Minister she
loved.

A charming incident which took place at Dr.
Morgan's diamond Jubilee meeting. Two
children from the Junior School came to the
platform, and one, addressing Dr. Morgan,
said :

" Our dear Dr. Morgan. We hope you will
forgive us for interrupting this programme, but
the Sunday School boys and girls have been
looking at it, and asking, ' Where do we come
in ? ' Then we decided that one boy and one
girl must come and say, ' Many happy returns of
your birthday,' and thank you very much for
making our School and Institute Halls look so
beautiful. We were not a bit afraid to come
into this great big meeting, because we know you
love boys and girls. People who like boys and
girls have a better sort of smile than the people
who don't. And you have got the proper smile.
Besides, we heard you say at our Anniversary

that 'the Church must always put Jesus and the child in the midst'. So we've come.

"Then just as we were coming, some ladies gave Bobbie this parcel to give to you, after I have read this letter loud enough for everybody to hear: 'Dear Dr. Morgan, Herein is a token of the loving good wishes of all present. We include everyone in the giving because we know so well how gladly they could have joined. But we could not make the intention public, and at the same time keep it a secret, and we thought of the two it would be better to keep it a secret, and so make it a surprise. So a few ladies in the congregation have contrived this gift in the name of all. It comes with loving prayers that God will give you health and strength long to continue the ministry of the Word at Westminster.'"

There was then handed to Dr. Morgan by the other child, a miniature of Mrs. Morgan, and the gift of a diamond brooch for Mrs. Morgan.

Dr. Morgan remarked once: "One of my deacons once said to me casually, lightly, smilingly, as though it was a pretty pleasing thing to say, 'Do you know, Mr. Morgan, I haven't seen my bairns (two beautiful children) awake for several months. You see I have been so fearfully busy I don't get home at night till they are in bed and on Sunday I am at the Church all day !' I said, ' My dear brother, for God's sake and the children's sake drop something in your business and if you can't do that, drop something in the Church and look after your bairns. They are the best investment you've got.' "

No son ever loved or looked after his father and mother better than Dr. Morgan did. When he first came to Westminster Chapel they came to live with him at Upper Norwood, and the death of his saintly father in 1907 was a great blow to him. I think that is a very remarkable photograph which shows Dr. Morgan surrounded by his own four sons, all five in ministerial dress. It was in 1888 that at Market Drayton he married Anne Morgan of Staunton, Gloucestershire, who through the long years has been the devoted partner in all his joys and anxieties. At the Diamond Jubilee meeting the veteran Dr. Charles Brown aroused a loud cheer by remarking with reference to Mrs. Morgan : " This congregation rises to that lady. If Elijah had had a sensible wife he would never have run away from Jezebel, and got under a juniper tree ! The ministry of the home has had a great deal to do with the ministry of this Church."

The longer one lives the more one wishes one could pay the tributes they deserve to the wives of our honoured ambassadors of Christ. But no ; they are hardly ever in the limelight. We hear comparatively little of them until they have done their work on earth. Then we may gain some little idea of what the loss has meant to those whom, in sunshine and in storm, they have so devotedly and unostentatiously cheered, encouraged and assisted. God bless them all !

CHAPTER IV

Dr. Morgan's Methods—Some Examples of his Style
—How he Builds up an Argument—His illustrations.

CHAPTER IV

Dr. Morgan is a Method-ist if ever there was one.

Mr. Harries tells us that a framed motto, " One with God is a majority", has had a prominent position in every study in which he, the doctor, has worked since he began his ministry.

He has almost a passion for system. He cannot bear unanswered letters or documents left about untidily. He believes in the most careful card indexing, filing, tabulating, cataloguing.

I cannot imagine him doing anything in a slovenly, slipshod way. I cannot imagine him selecting hymns for a service carelessly at the last moment (as some men do, to the disgust of their organists at least). He is sanely faddy about detail. One of the speakers we are heartily tired of is the man or woman who says : " I was wondering as I was coming along what I ought to talk about." Nothing of that sort about Campbell Morgan. He has not been dancing here, there, and everywhere rousing audiences by topical little extempores—the sort of man people speak of with a grin as " a good draw for our public meeting ". He has never lived with his head in the clouds, and he can talk as brightly as any other human being on the affairs of the day : but he is always happiest in exposition—the thing that has to be carefully, laboriously, prayerfully worked out in the study and presented in such a way that the hungry shall not be entertained, but fed.

How often, as a journalist, I have envied Dr. Morgan his power of using clean, plain, forcible English. Our temptation, and that of many a young preacher, is to search for high sounding words and phrases. I am going to remember and profit by what the doctor says about a review of a book of his that complained there were " no flowers of speech, no beauties of expression ". He tells us he cut out the criticism and pasted it in a book with the remark : " Lord, help me to keep right there." Rhetoric can be a delightful stimulant. It has been the plainest of speech, in the experience of most of us, that has convicted hearers and brought them to the feet of the Master Who wasted not a word.

The doctor can enjoy a jest, and he has an extensive repertoire of amusing stories, but these do not intrude in his public discourses. If he reminds students not to dwell too much upon one phase of truth, he does tell one story which is well worth quoting. A good Baptist preacher gave out the text, " Adam, where art thou ?" and said : " There are three lines we shall follow this morning. First we shall consider where Adam was. Secondly, we shall consider how he was to be got from where he was. Thirdly, and lastly, a few words about Baptism !" Dr. Morgan has no King Charles's head of that sort !

I used to hear occasionally a very independent London preacher who died some years ago. He drew large congregations. What is said of him now ? The writer of an autobiography who was closely associated with him says : " His beliefs were simply other names for his wishes. Voltaire is credited with the saying that in the beginning God made man in His own image, and man had returned the compliment by making God in his. ——certainly did this, and he made his Christ also."

Such a thing will never be said of Dr. Morgan. Principal Wheeler Robinson has defined a good sermon as that which utters the personal conviction of a great truth intelligibly expressed and applied, and imparted with the dignity of the Word of God, it must deal with great truths and not with trivialities; it must sound the note of conviction, it must belong to the unity we call worship, or "worthship".

Is not that exactly the kind of sermon Dr. Morgan preaches?

He believes in having a text, defining his theme. He thinks that if a man quotes a text at the beginning of his sermon and then wanders miles away from it he is not preaching, he is just talking.

The preacher's words, Dr. Hutton has said, "may be supported by the display of learning, by appeals to history, or by argument with men on their own ground. I make bold to say they are never really quickened and made powerful by such things. Preaching at its best does not argue; it merely arrests, declares, reveals. It holds up a light by which you see for the first time what all the time was there ".

I have no doubt many preachers will study deeply what Dr. Morgan says in " Preaching " on originality and authority as essentials in a sermon, and on the true meaning of that word " originality ". Sometimes we say a preacher is " original " because he has indulged in what sounds a very clever theory or speculation. Perhaps he has given the discourse what we call " an original title ". Dr. Morgan does not believe in that sort of thing. He has no show-manship of any sort. Long ago he realised that the truly original preacher does not create truth, but develops it : does not invent or even dis-cover new truth, but apprehends it, interprets a revelation.

" Religion," as Dr. W. B. Selbie says, " is suffering to-day, as so often in the past from the lack of an open vision." The Word of the Lord is rare, and men find it easier to accept hearsay and tradition than to discover for themselves the authentic voice of God. In the priestly and the prophetic in religion the priestly always wins because it represents the way of safety and the line of least resistance. The craving for authority is natural and legitimate, but we must beware of satisfying it too easily. The final appeal must always be a " Thus saith the Lord ".

If Dr. Morgan is asked, How do you make your sermons ? he says : " Two things are vital, first personal, first-hand work on the text, and then all scholarly aids obtainable. I never take down a commentary until I have done the first-hand work and have made my outline. To turn to commentaries first is to create a second-hand mentality. I speak freely, from a brief most carefully prepared."

Is it not remarkable to look back more than sixty years and find that his first sermon was divided with Biblical references just as his sermons are now? Here is the outline :

Theme : Salvation. (1) A *great* Salvation (Hebrews ii. 3) ; (2) A *common* Salvation (Jude 3) ; (3) An *eternal* Salvation (Hebrews v. 9) ; (4) A *present* Salvation (2 Cor. vi. 2).

Here is a typical passage which gives his habit of presenting a clear-cut argument :

" The Bible does not give us a systematised Theology. It presents a person in whom we find the final key to Theology in all its departments. In *the* Man of the Bible we have the key to Theological interpretation. We may take the Man of Nazareth, the Man of the Galilean Lake, and the Judean Hills and the Samaritan high-roads, and from Him project lines into infinitude, and those lines will include God. Men everywhere are feeling after God. All the highest thinking outside the sphere of revelation has been an attempt to know God by an enlargement of Man. Man projected men into immensity and in doing so flung out into infinitude the monstrosities of imperfect humanity : and Baal, and Moloch, and Jupiter and Zeus— what were those gods but magnified men ? In the fullness of time God gave us His Man, and if from Him we project the lines, we find God."

Nearly forty years ago, when he was at New Court, Messrs. Morgan and Scott published a little volume of his sermons entitled *Life Problems*. There was one on the words " What is man ?" and the way in which it opened was thoroughly characteristic of this preacher's method.

" We shall, in the first place, consider the

problem, as stated. Secondly, we shall direct our attention to a close inspection of the problem and thirdly and lastly we shall endeavour to apply that problem to personal consciousness."

There is the note of the methodical teacher there. Or to give another example : " We shall deal with Environment firstly as a popular conception : secondly as a Divine revelation ; and then we shall discuss the relation of these views."

The tender note in his closing appeals may be indicated by this fine example :

" God in Christ bends over man in infinite pity, over man whom He created in His own image : and He says, Wilt thou be made whole ? I turn my back to the allurements of the side that leads to evil and to hunger and I say, O Nazarene, Thou hast conquered by an infinitude of love, and if out of the wreckage of my life Thou canst create character that abides, I give myself to Thee. I will to follow Thee. That path leads right on to the eternal rest. I choose in the pulpit, and you cannot help me. You must choose in the pew, and I cannot help you. God help preacher and people alike to choose aright !"

Dr. Morgan does not talk much about himself, unless any little incident that came into his mind furnished a useful illustration. Once he said : " I very well remember when I was married my father came into my house. He was a Puritan, and I used to think it was hard lines that he was. To-day I thank God for it. He came into my home soon after the wedding and looked around, peering into every room. Then, in his own peculiar way, he said to me : ' Yes, all very nice. But nobody will know walking through here whether you belong to God or to the devil' ! I went through the rooms again and I thought, He is quite right. We made up our minds at once that there should be no room in the house henceforth that had not some message in picture text or book for every visitor, which should tell them that we at any rate would serve the King."

Dr. Morgan has more than once quoted with relish a sermon dealing with the text : " They that have turned the world upside down have come hither also." A preacher of rare insight made use of three divisions : (1) The world is upside down anyhow ; (2) To turn it upside down, therefore, is to turn it right side up ; (3) *Let us get at it !*

Once the doctor conducted a mission at Crewe, and for a fortnight came into contact with men who worked in the locomotive shops. " It was a remarkable fact," he says, " that these men were not prepared to take for granted any single thing I said. Neither were they prepared to accept an ideal of life simply because it was the ideal of another man. With hard-headed shrewdness they followed me as I dealt with them and not until they were clearly con-vinced of the reasonableness of the plan of salvation and of its actual suitability to their known needs were they prepared to make any confession of faith. They spent six days of the week in doing work that could not be loosely performed. Every small piece of the machinery of these majestic engines had perfectly to complement and fit its neigh-bours. There was exactitude in these men's lives for six days, and when they began to touch spiritual verities they brought to their study the same precision of observation that they applied to the work that their hands undertook."

I think I am right in saying that the closely reasonable clear-cut arguments of a man like Dr. Morgan would appeal to such men where a more emotional or sentimental speaker might fail. He was never after dramatic effect : always after securing a verdict on the *facts*.

How arrestingly he can bring out unsuspected meaning in a common word which we have passed by hundreds of times without a thought !

I will give one instance. One Sunday Dr. Morgan was talking about Hezekiah, and came to the words, " Like a swallow or a crane, so did I chatter." He had something to say about that little word " chatter ". " Dwellers in the country know something of what it is to hear the chatter of the birds, and indeed we can hear it in London, pigeons, sparrows, and starlings chattering. Did the King refer to his chatter as being something meaningless, devoid of all intelligence ? By no means. No one can imagine that if anything is really known about birds. We may be unable to understand the coo of the dove, or the chirp of the sparrow, or the strident note of the starling : but neither is meaningless. Perhaps if we had the understanding of St. Francis, or of Gipsy Smith, we might understand the chatter of the birds better than we do. I make no apology in declaring that God understands. It is never meaningless. It is not wholly ignorant. It is full of feeling. Hezekiah, therefore, takes the figure, as another prophet did, perhaps a little later, when Jeremiah said, not of the chatter, but of the birds : ' Yea, the stork in the heaven knoweth her appointed times ; and the turtle and the swallow and the crane observe the time of their coming.' Jeremiah knew that the birds were not ignorant, and Hezekiah knew that their chatter was not meaningless."

So Dr. Morgan went on to point out some of the things about which Hezekiah had been " chattering ", illuminating every passage, and concluded : " Someone is conscious at the moment of dark and desolate experiences, of disappointed hopes, and desolate life. All self-confidence is gone. To such I would say, Do not be afraid to chatter. Talk to God. Tell Him what you are feeling, resting assured that to anyone who does that, God will speak."

"His argument," said the late C. Silvester Horne of Dr. Morgan, "grows up so powerfully beneath his practised hand that at last one feels overwhelmed by it: there is no option but to consent." It has been with him the habit of a lifetime to consult a dictionary when dealing with a word. He always has one at his elbow. For example, he talked on the Romance of the Bible. He became critical of the word used in that way. He found in the dictionary romance could mean not only "to exaggerate" but "a blending of the heroic, the marvellous, the mysterious and the imaginative in actions, ideas, manners, languages, or literature." Then, he said, he felt safe.

The doctor has said that he has no right to speak as an expert in philosophy, but for forty years he had browsed in its fields always with great delight, and speaking from such knowledge he affirms that all human philosophy beginning with Anaxagoras, continuing through the first three living centuries, and then proceeding through those comparatively dead two millen-

niums until it blazed into life again with Bacon
and Descartes, on down to James and Dewey—
all human philosophy begins with Pilate's question when he stood confronting Jesus : What is
truth ?

It is interesting, by the way, to note that
Dr. Morgan strongly disagreed with Bacon
when he says Pilate was jesting. " He was
not. He was baffled. Life looked at him as
never before. He looked into the eyes of
Jesus and asked the greatest question of all."
Biblical philosophy, however, says the doctor,
does not begin with a question, but with an
affirmation.

Like most other great preachers, he has never
been content to draw his illustrations from his
library shelves. As he has travelled he has been
observant, and impressions received, freshened
many a sermon. He has, indeed, a genius
for illustration. Let me give one from a
sermon :

" There is in front of us a garden, well watered,
carefully tilled, properly tended. The soil is
rich and fertile. I hold in my hand two things :
a pebble that I have picked from the sea-shore
and an acorn that has just been shaken from

the oak by autumn's blast. I suppose for the moment that I do not know the nature of these two things. They are about the same size. They are not unlike in appearance. I put the pebble in the garden; I put the acorn in the garden. The environment is the same in both cases, the soil is the same, and the same sun with shafts of light will penetrate the soil and the same soft showers will reach the pebble and the acorn.

"You have already solved my riddle. The acorn will burst its shell in Spring, and we pass rapidly over the intervening centuries, and there it stands a proud oak battling against the blasts of winter, and in its turn shedding acorns to the ground. Where is the pebble? No one has disturbed its resting place. There was in it no germ of life. In God we live and move and have our being! There is no exception. Life to one man means growth, advancement, movement even on until that man is as a tree planted by the rivers of water. The other man living in the same environment is unmoved thereby. In him the spirit life is dead. The physical basis is there, but that never consciously touches God. The spirit neglected, starved, is dead. He is dead in his trespasses and sins. . . ."

Here is a characteristic story from a sermon :

" I remember one early morning as far back as 1887—years ago ! I had been out all through the night sitting by the bedside of a dying man in the city of Hull, and as I was making my way home, having seen him pass away, about four o'clock in the morning, turning suddenly around a corner I came face to face with a young fellow, the son of godly people, a child of tender care and constant prayer and yet who having fallen was just going the pace in wickedness. There was no escape, so he and I stood face to face. He was hurrying home through the grey morning after a night of carousal. I took his hand and said, ' Charlie, when are you going to stop this kind of thing ?' I shall never forget to my dying day what that man said and how he said it. He was about my own age at the time. Yet he was prematurely aged with sunken cheek and blood-shot eyes. Holding out a trembling hand he said : ' I would lose that hand here and now if only I knew how to stop.' I knew that was no isolated case. I am still more firmly convinced now that if only you could get the truth from young men who are going wrong it would be: 'I long to be pure. I hate impurity.'"

Here is another little story which he used with effect:

"I went to Douglas in the Isle of Man, and in one of my meetings a young lady came who said: 'All the joy had gone out of my life four years ago.' 'Praise God,' I said. 'What about?' said she. 'That you know when it went, because if you know when it went you know how it went.' She said, 'I don't think I do.' 'Yes, you do. You are very definite about the time. Now go back four years, and tell me what happened.' She hung her head for a while and I knew that something had happened. 'What was it?' She replied, 'I disagreed with my oldest friend. We were both Christians, and I wanted to tell her I was wrong but I did not, and she has left the country.' 'Well,' I said, 'write and tell her you were wrong. That is what the Master wanted you to do then. You will not otherwise get back the joy.' She fought God for twelve months about that letter, but when I next met her she said she had given in, and as the letter dropped into the letter box, heaven came back to her heart."

Once more I hear the authentic note of the evangelist :

"I was conducting a mission, and at the back of the Chapel sat a man to whom I came as I went around speaking to the people. I had been inviting them to come to the inquiry room. This man said, 'Can't I be saved without going in there?' Now when a man begins to ask that question you must deal with him just in one way. I said. 'No, I don't think you can.' 'Why?' he said. 'Is salvation in the inquiry room?' 'No, it is in God, but just as long as you sit here and want to dictate terms to God you are proving that you have not got to the end of self, and there is no salvation for you.' 'Then,' he said, 'if I can't be saved without going into that room, I'll go to hell.' 'My brother,' I said, 'that is not God's choice for you. If you choose it for yourself I cannot help it.'

"I warned the workers not to talk to that man, but to leave him alone. Every night he came and sat there. I said, 'Let God have His way with him.' I shall never forget the last night of the Mission. That man came forward

before I had time to ask a soul to move. I said,
' I thought you were going to hell, my brother.'
He said, ' Oh, I've been there all the week !'
Praise God, it does a man good to get there a
little while that way sometimes."

CHAPTER V

Some typical sayings—The supremacy of Christ—What coming to Christ means—Antagonism to God.

CHAPTER V

READING Dr. Morgan's sermons again and again I have thought : " I can imagine just how he said that, but what a lot is missing in cold print !" There are some preachers who say many things worth reading and re-reading. But a flash of the eye, a sudden raising of the voice, a vivid gesture, a scornful little laugh, a radiant smile—these are missing in the volume. How much the stay-at-homes will catch them through the medium of television I do not know.

I should like to give, however, one or two of Dr. Morgan's trenchant sayings culled from various sources. For example :

" Scholastic examinations are really no test of what a man knows. It is true in every department of life that the test fore-announced and prepared for, sometimes by cramming, is often at fault when we want to know what a man is or knows. God never fore-announces His examinations. What you are flashes out when you do not know anyone is likely to be watching you critically. In the small things, in the little

details, in the commonplaces of life character
shines out.

"I never try to find out what a preacher is
when he is preaching. It is when he is at home
and when he thinks there is no one there critically
to survey that you can find out what he really
is. I never want to find out what a deacon is in
a deacon's meeting. You do sometimes, but that
is not the best time. The time to find that out
is on Monday, Tuesday, Wednesday, during
the week."

"If I merely discourse on comparative re-
ligions in the pulpit, I can do no shepherding
of lost sheep. If I am not sure whether after all
it is not better to leave those distant nations to
Confucius and Buddha and Zoroaster and the
rest of them, well then in God's name let me
stay at home! Unless we have looked into His
eyes and said, O King most wonderful, even
though as yet we do not understand all the
mystery of Thy Person, Thou art peerless, alone,
absolutely supreme; we had better keep our
hands off the lambs and off the sheep."

"What do I mean by 'coming to Christ'?
I mean: Answer the gleam of light that has
come to you concerning purity; answer the

call that is welling up in your own life, declaring
the beauty of the Christian ideal, suggesting
that you begin the high and noble enterprise
of rising to the higher life in the name of the
Christ. The doctrines of grace? No man was
ever yet saved by believing the doctrines of
grace. You will understand them by and by.
And you will never understand the doctrines of
grace perfectly, until you get to heaven. Thank
God for that. I glory in the infinite mystery of
incarnation and atonement, and the doctrines
of grace. Oh man, not by an intellectual appre-
hension of these doctrines is a man saved,
but by answering the light, yielding to the
immediate truth, giving myself to Christ as He
says Follow Me."

" The disciples of Jesus never come apart
to close dealing with the Master without something very like this happening. He begins to
talk to us ; we come face to face with things
that shame us in our own lives ; we come face
to face with Christ standing before us telling
us of His knowledge of the shameful thing and
telling us of His ability to deal with it for ever.
I am inclined to say we can measure our intimacy
with Him by these standards. If there has been

no such revelation I question whether I have been very near the Lord."

" Oh, the gospel of getting on ! I wish I could get rid of it for ever ! I pick up a book and I read : From Log Cabin to White House. I cast no shadow on Garfield but I do say his greatness was not proved by the fact that he left the log cabin and reached the White House. He was a great man in the cabin. If a man gets on and becomes mayor or President and thinks that is everything, it is a lie and the sooner those facing life get rid of such an idea the better."

" You say : Can't we improve the dwellings of the poor? Yes, God help us to do it. But one of the best ways is to improve the man that lives in the dwelling."

" It is said, we are not antagonistic to God. Think again and think carefully. People of whom we speak as cultured—I am not denying their culture or their refinement ;—people who even observe the outward ceremonies of religion, are antagonistic to God. They do not want to talk about God. There are places where, if you were invited to dinner, and you talked about God, you would never be invited again. I am not thinking of the men who are engaged in infidel propaganda. That is a harmless antagonism to God. I am thinking of the common and deep-rooted antagonism to God found in human nature. It is based on the fact that the human soul, alienated from God, does not know God."

"In Christ I find God. In Christ my heart learns to love God, and can do no other than love God. In Christ therefore I find the secret of the change in the output of energy that transforms my energy from hurtfulness to beneficence. You and I live with God, and walk with God, and talk with God, and have fellowship with God, through Jesus Christ."

"God is everywhere, in the sky, and air, and sea, and the trees, and the lake, and the birds, and the flowers; and yet we cannot find Him. Why not? We are alienated; and we are at enmity in mind, and all our life is expressed in that phrase, ' wicked works '."

"The most tremendous cry of the human heart is a cry after God. The most poignant sorrow of the human heart is lack of God. What is sorrow? Sorrow is a sense of lack, and the ultimate in all sorrow is lack of God. That is hell, and that will be hell. Christian souls are not saying, 'Oh that I knew where I might find Him.' We have found God in Jesus Christ."

"What is the Christian position with regard to the underworld? Conflict first. Do not forget that. Secondly, perfect equipment for the conflict. Thirdly, victory all the time if we will avail ourselves of our equipment. All this is plainly revealed in Ephesians. Conflict against the organised and massed forces of evil, which nevertheless are defeated. The rulers of this darkness we have to fight. But we have perfect equipment, we are under the rule of Christ; we proceed in the strength of Christ; we exercise the authority of Christ. With regard to our equipment we are given two commands. First, we are told to put on the armour of God. Then we are to take up the armour of God. Do not separate these.

" We are charged to put on the whole armour of God, or the panoply of God. What does that mean? It means: Put on the armour God wears. I am to be equipped in my conflict with Satan by the very armour which makes God invincible against the devil. The armour of God is made available to me in Christ. If we go out to meet this underworld of evil, panoplied in Christ, we cannot be beaten, we cannot be defeated; it will be victory all the way."

"Has it ever occurred to you that it may be that the fall of Satan was connected with the creation of man? I am not saying that it was so, but I have sometimes thought so. I have thought that there may be some warrant for the view that when the angels kept not their first estate, it was that their revolt against God was rebellion against His creating a higher order of being than themselves. I do not know."

"To deny the personality of Satan and the underworld of demon spirits, is the severest and most terrible indictment of humanity which it is possible to make. If there be no personal devil, if there be no spiritual underworld, according to the Bible revelation, then all the foul and black and dastardly and damnable things that blight the human race, have originated in human nature."

"There are many things of which I am perfectly certain by faith founded on reason which yet I cannot demonstrate to the logical satisfaction of any other person. I look into the face of my mother, and I know she is my mother by the activity of faith based upon reason. It is absolutely impossible to demonstrate the fact, but the evidence is overwhelming."

" Some men have dreamed wonderful dreams. In Edward Bellamy's books I detected the aspiration of a great heart after a divine ideal that he never understood. The trouble was Edward Bellamy wanted to get society into the kingdom of God without taking it by the way of the cross of Jesus Christ, and he could never do it. He and other dreamers of beautiful dreams in which men shall lose the miserable idea that any work is dishonourable wanted to pass into that realm outside the actual positive interfering government of God, and it can never be done.

" You cannot grow the tulips of the Kingdom of God except you get the bulbs from heaven. Never forget that."

" Sometimes as a child," he said once in a lecture at Fifth Avenue Church, " I remember I lay awake at nights trying to think of what *for ever* meant, until my childish brain nearly turned with dread. Such a thought still fills the soul with awe—the ages rolling one after another in majestic order. I know not what the ages will be, but they have lost their terror for me. This is the age of God's grace. It has lasted for nineteen hundred years. Presently it will end and beyond it—what? Who shall tell? I see the ages coming ever coming lit with their own distinctive glory all derived from the essential Being of Deity but they are fashioned by the Christ. Every new age shall receive its value, its new unfolding of the essential mystery of God, under His direction."

Speaking at Northfield nearly forty years ago, Dr. Morgan declared: "These are evil days. It is the age of rush, of movement, of effort. The old sacred art of contemplation and meditation is almost dead. It is the age when men and women are trying to live even within the Church by dissipating and exciting forms of so called religious services. The old solemn hours of quiet loneliness with God that made the saints of the past are almost unknown. We are carried up and borne forward before we know it upon the rush that characterises the time. When men and women come to me as they do sometimes and say we need in the Church to catch the spirit of the age and keep level with it, I say In God's name, No! What we need is to be led

by the Spirit of God, and that will send us against
the spirit of the age and never along with it."

If Dr. Morgan spoke thus in 1900, how much
more emphatically might he repeat the warning
in 1938! "The general atmosphere in which
we are surrounded," he added, "is against the
government of God. We may have our meetings
and sing the praises of what we have done and
where we have reached to, but I tell you that if
Jesus came back and preached the gospel He
preached in Jerusalem they would crucify Him
quicker than they did in Jerusalem. If He came
again with the same words, the same teaching,
the same statements of divine will and government He would find no room for Himself in the
very cities that bear the name of Christian to-
day. The most terrible thing is this, that while
men are against the government of God they
are praying, Thy Kingdom come, Thy will
be done.

"The most terrible blasphemy of the age is
not the blasphemy of the slums, but the blasphemy
of the place of worship where men pray such
prayers and then go out to deny every principle
of divine government in their lives."

CHAPTER VI

Dr. Morgan and Revival—" Special Missions "—Religious Films—Dr. Morgan's true Catholicism—His appeals for unity.

CHAPTER VI

I ONCE heard Dr. Morgan say, with a whimsical emphasis, that so far as he was personally concerned, he would be very glad to join an alliance that would promise not to publish any Church Statistics for ten years. Seriously, he did not think the true spiritual power of any Church was to be measured by statistics. But he deplored the lack of conversions. "I greatly grieve," he said, "When I am told that those who adhere to a particular Church conviction and order are not able to do the kind of work that belongs to the Salvation Army. I deny it absolutely. I thank God for the Salvation Army. But the work of winning individual men for Jesus Christ from every rank and social walk in life and society is the work of the whole Church, which should cease trifling, and close her ranks, and march forward."

He used to say he did not pray for "an old-fashioned revival". "I want God's next new thing," he said. "If a man is praying for an old-fashioned revival, in all probability when

God's visitation comes, he will not be conscious of it. Men remembering the marvellous movement under Finney might have prayed for an old-fashioned revival such as that which accompanied his preaching. It is more than likely that when God raised up Dwight L. Moody such men would be out of sympathy with all his methods for a long while, for the notes of the two movements were utterly different. God fulfils Himself in many ways. We ought to be so living that when God begins His great triumphant march we shall fall in with the first battalion and have part in the first victories."

Dr. Morgan has never encouraged unauthorised and unattached evangelising, even by individual members of the Church of Christ. He criticised no movement that acted independently of the Churches but said he had grave suspicion of anything that boasted it was undenominational. "I have," he said, "a very great love for everything that is inter-denominational which is quite another matter."

He has not thought it wise to hold an evangelistic service in a Church at stated intervals. "If I may refer to my own experience as a pastor,"

he has said, "I have gone on from Sunday to
Sunday sometimes for one or two months with
an evangelistic service after each evening service.
On the other hand, there have been periods
when only once in the month or perhaps twice
such services have been held and sometimes
months would pass with no such service. I
never went to my pulpit knowing whether I
should have such a service or not. I went with
a burden and a message, and have endeavoured
to lead and train my Church in co-operation
with me. They were never surprised if I had
an after meeting. . . . There is no congregation
made up of saints. There will be an element in
all congregations of those interested but not
submitted, and the minister must ever have on
his heart the burden of such people."

Dr. Morgan took a prominent part in the
simultaneous mission arranged by the National
Free Church Council. It was said by some
that it was a failure. Dr. Morgan said at least it
was a glorious success, in that it aroused in the
hearts of hundreds of pastors an interest in
evangelistic work and turned them to evangelism
in their own Churches. The provincial mission
which Dr. Morgan conducted at that time was

held in a Town Hall. At a Conference the ministers said, " What can we do to carry on the work ?" Dr. Morgan said, " Let every man, whether he has ever done so before or not, go and preach to his own congregation with the distinctive and avowed purpose of persuading many of those whom he loves but who have not as yet yielded to Christ to yield to Him at once." To this they agreed . . . and through all the city men and women were saved.

" In an evangelistic service," the doctor says, " the service must be aimed at the capture of the will for Jesus Christ. Different congregations will demand different methods. Thomas Champness says that the most remarkable text on how to be a soul winner is the text, ' I will make you fishers of men.' I once heard him speak on that text, and he said a fisherman is very careful about his bait. ' If I want to catch a codfish I fling them out a bait as big as a clock weight, and they swallow it. But if I am going for a salmon I have a fly and whip the stream with delicacy and art.'

"Whether the preacher captures the will through the intellect or through the emotion depends upon the persons addressed and on the preacher,

but the supreme business is to appeal to the will,
and to bring it into submission to the Lordship
of Christ."

Like the late Prebendary Webb Peploe and
the late Dr. F. B. Meyer, Dr. Morgan often dealt
when at Northfield with the subject of Scriptural
Holiness. There was no advocacy of "sinless
perfection", but a clear presentation of the
possibilities of a life truly yielded to God and
the privilege it afforded of living free from the
bondage of sin. I remember being with him for
a week at the famous Southport Convention,
a few years ago. He had not often attended these
tent meetings but he gave the morning Bible
reading to the intense delight of those present,
and frequently expressed his own pleasure at
hearing the rousing Methodist singing.

Samuel Chadwick, who had had so much
to do with the success of this old-established
Convention, was one of his oldest friends.
They had very much in common. Both had a
passionate love for the Bible, and both found
their chief delight in expounding it. Both
believed with all their hearts in evangelism. Both
had the saving grace of humour. Dr. Morgan
for many years had the little paper *The Joyful*

News sent to him, and read every word that his friend Chadwick had written therein.

When *The Christian* recently took up the question of film services, Dr. Morgan wrote to the Editor : " I want to place myself on record as being in absolute agreement with everything you have written. The perils which you see are certainly there. You say that when a film is substituted for a sermon it may easily be interpreted by the public as a confession of the bankruptcy of the pulpits. So far as I am concerned, that exactly expresses the truth."

Dr. Morgan had seen a film called *Triumph*, and agreed that while much in it was attractive, the presentation of our Lord was repellent. " I do not mean that it was not reverent," he said, " but that any representation that must inevitably fall so short of the truth of the Personality is out of place. Moreover, there were some ridiculous inaccuracies and mixtures in the narrative. I still believe that the method of the Gospel is the method of preaching."

Though I have no recollection of hearing him say much on the subject, I do not think Dr. Morgan has ever been anxious to enter into argument as to the claims of Spiritists. I do remember him saying, when speaking of the raising of Lazarus, that he was going to indulge in no wild speculations. He spoke of death as a sleep. " Sleep," he said, " is not a cessation of being. It is an unconsciousness of all things around. I am not going to suggest that our loved ones know what we are doing here. There may be certain circumstances in which, in the government of God, they are permitted to see and know. As a rule, so far as we are concerned, they are asleep. Aren't you rather glad for their sakes that that is so ? I am. . . . I say emphatically no other voice than that of Jesus could have reached that young man Lazarus."

Speaking of the revolt against materialism, Dr. Morgan once quoted as some evidence the growth of Christian Science, which, travelling about the world, he found successful everywhere. " I hold Christian Science," he said plainly, " to be characterised by an absence of the Christian and an ignorance of Science. What is the secret ? It says, there is no material, everything is spiritual, and this very emphasis of the spiritual has been the attraction of a people tired of materialism. . . . I do not hesitate to affirm that if the Christian Church had only

been true to the gospel of spirituality and the
gospel of holiness, there would have been no
room for Christian Science. Though the latter
is but a will-o'-the-wisp dancing among the
quagmires men would rather have the will-o'-the-
wisp than the dense black darkness of materialism."

"Sometimes," Dr. Morgan once said, " I
am asked what Church I belong to. When I
reply, I am a Catholic Churchman, I have seen
people look surprised. Yet that is exactly what
I am. The Catholic Church is of course the
whole Church, such a phrase as Roman Catholic
is a contradiction in terms."

His maternal grandfather was a deacon of the
Baptist Church of Upwell, near Downham, in
Norfolk. His father was a Baptist Minister who
gave up Church and salary. He was very largely
in sympathy with the views of Plymouth Brethren,
having been drawn by the influence of
those saints of Western England—Robert Chap-
man and George Müller. Holding the doctrine of
the pre-millennial coming of Christ the pastor
surrendered worldly prospects in order to follow
the dictates of conscience.

Dr. Morgan has always been truly Catholic.
His friend Dr. Hulme says : " I have often had

to visit our little Church at Monmouth, and I know well that little schoolroom where Dr. Morgan preached his first sermon from the desk that has now found a resting-place in Westminster Chapel. If that desk could speak it 'could a tale unfold' that would stir the hearts of us all. It is now forty years since he came to conduct a week's mission at my Church at Jesmond, Newcastle-on-Tyne. Unfortunately influenza laid him low in the middle of the week, and I had to take the remaining Services myself.

" A few years later I was lecturing at a down-town Church near the Cardiff Docks, and just after I began to talk on ' The romance of yester-day and the call of to-day ', in walked Campbell Morgan with his intimate friend, Frank Fifoot. I realised at once I then had the opportunity of retaliating. So, after talking for twenty minutes on the romance of the past, I said ' I will now ask my friend, Dr. Campbell Morgan, to give the second half of this lecture on " the call of to-day ".' Immediately I sat down, to the great delight of the audience, and quite unperturbed, my friend came forward and for half an hour talked on the subject allotted to him to the great edification and satisfaction of the audience."

In recent days we have heard a great deal about the union of the Churches. Dr. Morgan is a Vice-President of the World's Evangelical Alliance, and long ago he was urging the need of Christian Union. On what foundation must it, in his opinion, be based? First, the Divine origin, Authority and sufficiency of the Holy Scriptures. (He prefers the word " origin " to the word " inspiration ".) He growingly felt that he could have no long-continued communion or fellowship in Christian work with those who could not stand on that platform.

He has asked: " Do you get any comfort out of the division in the Church of God? I hope you don't. I hope you have never said it is part of the Divine plan that Christendom should be split into a thousand fragments. I tell you it isn't. Jesus said, ' I will that they may be one that the world may know that Thou hast sent me.' We are not manifestly one and that is why the world doesn't know that God sent Jesus."

" Do you know a man that casts out devils, brother, in the Presbyterian Church, and he isn't a Presbyterian? Don't hinder him. Supposing he is none of your ists or isms, supposing he is a man who has got into touch with Christ but hardly knows the truth himself yet. Let him alone. He cannot work a work in the name of Christ and speak evil of Him. If he is not against Christ, he is with Him."

He wrote once that he saw the peril of narrowness. He also saw the peril of breadth, and was more afraid of it. " If we are to be broad enough to include the things that destroy," he said, " I for one shall hark back to the narrowness of an older day. If there is to be any comprehension that makes room for tendencies towards Rome, then," he exclaimed, " I have but one watchword,—a barred door to Popery and no peace with Rome."

Again he remarked, " So far as we feel that the Rationalistic treatment that calls in question the supernatural and the miraculous and inevitably and logically ends in the denial of the Resurrection itself, cannot be taken into the fellowship of endeavour, then it seems to me there is no reason why the Christian Churches should not join their ranks in the interests of the world and its wide open doors."

When the doctor responded to the call to East Northfield soon after the death of D. L. Moody, he had just declined a call to the Fifth

Avenue Presbyterian Church in New York, but he explained that he felt this case was different. He had long felt that God was preparing him for a Ministry to the Churches, rather than to one particular Church.

"I go," he said simply, "to preach the English Bible, to speak in different centres out of the Book of God. I know one or two things the Bible says, and others I am beginning to find out. When I read the story of one called Adam I find that man, God-created, is never forsaken. In the story of Abraham, I find that man, God-guided, is always led into possession. In the story of Moses, I find that man, God-instructed, is never ignorant. In the story of David I find that man, God-like, sings through his own failure till the glorious triumph comes. These are only notes of the music that I find in the Book."

And that glorious music has so little, after all, to do with our poor little denominational labels.

At Westminster early in 1938 Dr. Morgan preached a series of Sunday evening sermons on Church Unity. He began with the words, "One body, one spirit, one vocation." His first word was that his procedure would not be polemic but expository. He did not like the word " polemic ". That meant war, and there was no war in his heart. He quickly came to the question : " What is the one vocation of the Church," and exclaimed : " You know it, and hear it *ad nauseam*, but hear it again. The age-long, eternal business of the Church is to reveal God. The one thing that is the matter with the world is that it has turned from God, and does not know God. The vocation of the Church is to reveal the grace of God, and when the world sees God as He is, then men and women every-where will be heard saying, O God, who would not give his heart to Thee ! "

When he gave the first of those addresses Dr. Morgan, before leaving home, had been " lis-tening-in " to the Archbishop of York. " I felt," he said, " how completely he and I were one in the great essentials." His points were put with all his usual clarity in due order just as a professor might talk to his students, as in suc-cessive addresses he dealt with the great subject uncontroversially under such headings as " Vision ", " Realisation ", " Methods ", " Re-sponsibility ", " The ultimate victory ". I hope the whole will be printed and that many will be able closely to study the conclusions on this vital question of one so eminently qualified to offer counsel and guidance.

This man's whole life, however, has been a sermon on true unity and brotherhood. Just before I wrote this I saw him taking part in a gathering of friends of Wesley's Chapel, in which historic building he has always taken the deepest interest. On several Sunday evenings when his doctor has not allowed him to preach he has been seen fully appreciating hearty services and good sermons in churches of various denominations. How much the appreciation of such an encourager means to them!

CHAPTER VII

The Doctor's Own reminiscences—His diamond jubilee—
He sums up his own endeavour.

CHAPTER VII

I SEEM to remember Dr. Morgan saying once
with regard to May meetings that he almost
felt like starting a Society for the abolition of
all Societies. Certainly the unnecessary over-
lapping that exists is scandalous. I do not think he
has ever cared to be prominently associated with
many societies, however good their objects.
He has had his own work, and has stuck to it;
never seeking to be President of this and vice-
President of that, and a leading speaker at
anniversary meetings. I have heard him make
charming little speeches when brethren who
were his friends were being honoured, but he
will not be remembered as an orator, or as a
popular platform man. You might as well
expect the Governor of a College to be noted
for his amateur theatricals.

Very rarely has he talked of himself. Towards the end of 1936 an attractive lantern
lecture was given at Westminster Chapel by the
well-known photographer, Mr. Walter Stone-
man, and somehow Dr. Morgan, who presided,

was actually prevailed upon to give twenty minutes to "Reminiscences". I look at my shorthand notes and marvel at the interesting material he crowded into that short time. He began with a memory of the home at Cardiff during the years 1870 and 1871.

"In that room," he said, "I first preached. I had one living person in my audience, and quite a number that were not alive. I preached regularly there week after week and time after time to my sister and her dolls. It was then that there was born within me the passion to become a preacher.

"My father was a preacher, and, I do not hesitate to say, a great preacher. My greatest joy in those days was to go with him to hear other preachers. I think most of those I heard were Methodist preachers, which may account for much, although my father was not a Methodist. The names that come back to me are those that will not be known probably to many : Richard Roberts, Morley Punshon, Gervase Smith, Mr. Rattenbury, the grandfather of Dr. J. Ernest Rattenbury. I also clearly remember hearing Newman Hall. Across the years I remember the keen delight with which I used to listen.

It was thus that the passion for preaching took possession of me."

He spoke of his first sermon, the circumstances under which he left the Jewish school, to which I have referred. " So," he continued, " I found myself thrust out. I had no resources. I had had to give up the idea of going to the University. I had no money with which to go to any theological institution. I have never been to one. I have been the President of one—but perhaps that needs no special training ! "

Dr. Morgan was Principal of Cheshunt College, Cambridge, for three years. " I went forth," he continued, " into the evangelistic field. I took my first series of meetings for a week, conducting two meetings a day. I was entertained happily and comfortably in a home. At the end of the week my host gave me an envelope and said, ' Your travelling expenses are there and anything over you will keep for yourself.' The expenses totalled 4s. 7d. for a return ticket from Birmingham. The whole contents of the envelope was the sum of ten shillings ! "

He mentioned his evangelistic work in connection with the Methodist Church. " I had joined them," he said, " because of their love

and passion for evangelism, although I had not
been born or born again in that Communion.
In the midst of my evangelistic work, a Congregational Church at Stone in Staffordshire asked
me to become their minister. I accepted the invitation and thus entered the ministry by irregular
methods. The Holy Spirit often does irregular
things that are nevertheless regular in the
economy of God.

"I owe my acceptance by the Congregational
Union to Dr. Charles Berry. My ministry then
began at Stone, rightly named so far as my
experience is concerned. Rugeley, a happy
smaller country Church with a loving band
that gave me time for reading and thought.
Thence I passed to Birmingham, the Westminster Road Church in Handsworth in '93,
where I spent a happy time. Then in '97 to
New Court, London."

Having spoken of his coming to Westminster,
and the many years he spent in the States, Dr.
Morgan concluded: "My last reminiscence is
that of a visit to England in 1932, a quiet talk
in a beautiful study with Hubert Simpson, too
sacred to say much about, and I came back. I
may and will say that nothing would have

brought me back other than that talk with him, a saint of the Most High, by whose side it was a joy to stand. I came, desiring to help him."

In November, 1936, came the celebration of his diamond jubilee as a preacher. In that same year two other outstanding men attained their diamond jubilee—Dr. J. Scott Lidgett and Dr. Dinsdale Young. "Dr. Morgan," says Dr. Ferrier Hulme, "would have been a Methodist minister, too, but for the interposition of one or two of his intimate friends, who were not as wise and far-seeing as they thought they were. However, God has His own way of over-ruling the mistaken judgment of man, and causing it to turn out for the greater good of His Church."

At the great Diamond Jubilee Meeting, Lord Craigmyle, who presided, said: "Come with me into the circle of my intimate friendships. My hearers, one of God's greatest mercies to me has been that He has chosen for me among my most valued friends in life, great divines; eminent, scholarly, truly spiritually-minded and profoundly reverent men, to company with whom was a veritable inspiration. Shall I make so free as to recall from among them three great souls ? Robert Rainy ; my heart burns within me when I pronounce his name ; Alexander Whyte, the father of many spiritual children still living on his teaching, and cherishing his memory ; Fairbairn, of Oxford, whose eloquence was like a searching flame. These three men, mighty in Scriptures, march in my mind and memory through the years. In these latest happy times they march not three, but four deep. Who is the fourth divine ? I declare he is their kindred spirit and of the same enriching and accomplished quality of friendship and of mind. His name is Campbell Morgan."

Dr. John Hutton said London was in no doubt as to the quality of Dr. Morgan. " He stands for what men are coming to see they desperately need. He has obeyed the Pauline instruction and example : One thing I know, and one thing I do." Dr. Sidney Berry spoke in warm affectionate terms for the Congregational Church, and the Rev. C. Ensor Walters, the President, for the Methodist Church ; Dr. Charles Brown for the Baptist Church.

How brief and simple was Dr. Morgan's reply to all the good things that had been said about him : " I notice how all my brethren have claimed me, and that is a great joy," he said. "I have been a Methodist Local Preacher. I am a thoroughly convinced and unrepentant Congregationalist ecclesiastically. I have had the joy of being a Presbyterian minister, and I have been brought up in my early years in Baptist surroundings.

"Looking back over the sixty years, to quote the Psalmist's words, if I am a wonder unto many, I am a greater wonder to myself. I am an on-looking man, and am far more concerned with the great future than with the past, that whatever remains of service should be to the glory of Him Whom I love and have tried to preach through the sixty years. I thank God for the sixty years, in which God has never failed me."

In a recent sermon which I heard at Westminster, Dr. Morgan had a question to ask, though he said he tried to get away from it, and somebody ought to answer it. In the new *Bible as Literature* he can understand why the genealogies have been left out, but why, Oh why, he asked, have the wise-acres who prepared it left out the Letter to the Ephesians? "If anybody can explain," he said, "let them come and see me, but don't let them come guessing, for I can do all the guessing that is necessary ! "

No ! No one has ever expected guess-work at Westminster Chapel. The veteran preacher has expounded, in many volumes, practically the whole of the Bible. He would gladly go on doing it for another sixty years. And as he flashes his torch on this word and that, the man is forgotten in the wonder of the Book and the beauty of his Lord.

When, years ago, Dr. Morgan was bidden God-speed on his first departure for Northfield, Dr. Joseph Parker said in his presence : " The one ministry that will last and be as fresh at the end as it was at the beginning is a Biblical and an expository one. Mere anecdotes fail and exhaust themselves ; the word of the Lord abideth for ever."

I think here of the poet Cowper's ideal preacher :

> Would I describe a preacher . . .
> I would express him simple, grave, sincere,
> In doctrine uncorrupt, in language plain,
> And plain in manner, decent, solemn, chaste,
> And natural in gesture ; much impressed
> Himself, as conscious of his awful charge,

And anxious mainly that the flock he feeds
May feel it too ; affectionate in look,
And tender in address, as well becomes
A messenger of grace to guilty men.

" I have endeavoured to speak the things I *know*," says Dr. Morgan himself. " I have many doubts, I have many questionings. There are certain departments of theological thought in which I find myself utterly at sea. I never take them into the pulpit. Sometimes the truths I have tried to teach have all been expressed in one of the sweetest verses in the whole realm of hymnology :

"I worship Thee, sweet Will of God,
And all Thy ways adore,
And every day I live I seem
To love Thee more and more."

What is there one can add to that ? Nothing at all. Except that we who owe him so much pray that his life of praise may be prolonged, and that at eventide it may be very light.

THE END